The Natural Waterways
of Great Britain

Also by Michael and Laura Murphy

Vacation Rentals in Europe: A Guide
*The Natural Waterways of Ireland: A Traveler's Guide to
Rental Boating*

Other Interlink Titles of Interest

American Walks in London
Edinburgh: A Cultural and Literary Companion
The Independent Walker's Guide to Great Britain
London for Families
London for Lovers
Oxford: A Cultural and Literary Companion
A Traveller's History of England
A Traveller's History of London
A Traveller's History of Scotland
Wild Britain

The Natural Waterways of Great Britain

A Traveler's Guide to Rental Boating

by Michael and Laura Murphy

Interlink Books

An imprint of Interlink Publishing Group, Inc.
New York • Northampton

First published 2000 by

INTERLINK BOOKS
An imprint of Interlink Publishing Group, Inc.
99 Seventh Avenue • Brooklyn, New York 11215 and
46 Crosby Street • Northampton, Massachusetts 01060
www.interlinkbooks.com

Copyright © by Michael and Laura Murphy 2000

Library of Congress Cataloging-in-Publication Data

Murphy, Michael, 1927–
   The natural waterways of Great Britain : a traveler's guide to rental
boating / by Michael and Laura Murphy
      p.   cm.
   ISBN 1-56656-346-1 (pbk. : alk. paper)
   1. Boats and boating--Great Britain Guidebooks 2. Waterways--Great
Britain Guidebooks. 3. Great Britain Guidebooks.
   I. Murphy, Laura.   II. Title.
GV776.43.A2M87   1999
914.104'859--dc21   99-39155

Printed and bound in Canada

To request our complete 44-page full-color catalog,
please call us toll free at **1-800-238-LINK,** visit our
website at **www.interlinkbooks.com**, or write to
Interlink Publishing
46 Crosby Street, Northampton, MA 01060
e-mail: info@interlinkbooks.com

CONTENTS

PREFACE

A few years ago we were journeying through Great Britain working on a guidebook to vacation rentals in Europe. Our first stop after London was in the little town of Wroxham, Norfolk, a few miles north of the Cathedral city of Norwich, itself a little over a hundred miles northeast of London. The modern brick townhouse we stayed in faced a strip of grass and a row of small trees that bordered a concrete quay which, in turn, bordered a broad, slow-moving river. To our right along the concrete dock about a dozen motor launches were tied, along with half a dozen sailboats. Although the boats were of various sizes and configurations, all flew the same flag insignia. We thought they might belong to members of a yacht club.

A young woman was cleaning a handsome motor cruiser that we judged to be some forty feet in length. To pass the time of day we enquired about the boats and the yacht club. The boats, we were astonished to learn, were not the pleasure craft of the well to do, they were for rent—for "hire" as the British say. Hire cruisers available by the week (or "short-breaks" in the off-season) to anyone over eighteen years old who could pay the price and could see well enough to drive. Nothing was required: no license and no experience. Even the price was surprisingly modest, less than the price of a room in a decent London hotel. When we asked if they would actually turn over one of these $100,000 motor cruisers to us, we who had no motor boating experience, the reply was yes, indeed. We had always thought that canals and narrowboats were fun, a little "restrictive" perhaps, but here was something better: open waters and more freedom to go wherever one wished.

How would we learn about operating one, we asked. How would we find out where to go? They would spend an hour or so with us, we were told, until we felt comfortable with what we were about to do. They would show us the switches and how to steer and tie up, go over the few rules, look at the charts and point out the many other boatyards along the routes, talk about safety, mention favorite pubs and inns and towns along the routes, help us select an itinerary if we wished, show us the pots, pans, dinnerware and bedding, cruise around a bit, demonstrate how to operate forward and reverse, tie the right knots at the moorings, and answer questions. She said no one traveled at high speed—these were tranquil journeys. They would suggest where to buy groceries in Wroxham. But not too many, she said—there are towns and shops along the way. And then they would hand us the keys.

We looked across the slow-moving water of the River Bure and wondered aloud what sort of world actually lay out of sight beyond the trees cradled in the river's nearest bend. It's the Norfolk Broads, the woman explained, a national parkland, an expansive area of lakes and rivers, fens and forests, swans and grebes, castles and windmills, owls and harriers, market towns, abbeys and waterside pubs, occupying much of Norfolk County. We were told that some boaters took rented bicycles along to explore forest and marshland paths, and some towed a skiff in order to explore more shallow coves and backwaters.

We also learned that boats are available not only on the broads and rivers of East Anglia, but on the Thames from London westward for a hundred and twenty five miles through the heart of England, in Cambridgeshire, on Lake Windermere, on the Avon, the Yorkshire Ouse, the long chain of lakes of the Scottish Highlands, and Ireland's Shannon-Erne (the subject of our second book in the series).

The Broads beckoned, but we were on a land-bound four month itinerary and could not sail off into the Norfolk sunrise. It remained in our thoughts, however, knowing that the vast waterlands were there, and that the boats were waiting. Large cruisers and small, modest and luxurious.

Later, traveling through the southwest of France, we spotted two cabin cruisers idling along the River Lot near the ancient city of Cahors, and found that they were among the many cabin cruiser rentals that are now appearing on rivers that flow through some of the most picturesque regions of France.

Later still we read of the re-opening of a canal in Ireland that again connected the headwaters of the Republic's River Shannon with the River Erne and the Erne lakes of Northern Ireland's County Fermanach, forming the longest waterway in Europe open to pleasure boating. The enjoyment of cruising rivers and lakes, it seemed, was catching on, spreading from the Norfolk Broads, where it started nearly a century ago when a certain Harry Blake began offering sailing yachts and shallow-hulled sailing wherries for rent, attracting city folks who came from London, Norwich, Manchester, and beyond for "Boating Holidays on the Broads."

The idea of exploring countrysides both familiar and new from the vantage of a slow-moving cabin cruiser became reality when a magazine assignment took us to Ireland's River Shannon, where on a rented thirty-foot cabin cruiser we pushed off for one of the most stimulating and gratifying weeks of our lives.

Upon leaving Ireland we spent a week on the Southern Broads, where it became obvious that few Americans knew about these vast natural lake and river systems of Europe, much less how to explore them. That, we felt, needed to be remedied, so we returned once more and began a water odyssey, a great near-circle during which we operated a variety of cruisers on all the important natural waterways of Britain and Ireland, from the estuary of the Shannon to the lakes of Scotland, a return to the Broads, and ended over two months later near the headwaters of the Thames. From this, from study and from past travels has emerged two waterway guides, logically divided between the island that is Britain and the island that is Ireland.

Of final note, it is essential to understand that nothing happens fast on the British and Irish waters, where the leisure boat speed limit there is rarely over six miles per hour. As we wrote in our first article on the subject, "This is lying-back, bird-watching, castle-viewing, photo-taking territory. A place to restore the soul."

We anticipate that this guide will offer readers the means to see new sights, to see old sights from a new perspective, to experience a different way of travel, to savor the rich rewards of the waterways.

Michael and Laura Murphy

CHAPTER 1

The Search for a European Getaway

I t has become increasingly difficult for vacationers and other travelers to find some desirable spot relatively free from the tourist crowds. The inventiveness of those in the travel trade, along with the affluence and mobility of the traveling public, has made formerly exotic destinations easy to reach. And on arrival, they are often disappointingly full of fellow visitors. Operators can be found to take tour groups onto the ice of Antarctica, to the jungles of the Amazon, across the Pampas, or into the seamier sections of Bangkok. Money can buy privacy and exclusivity, but for the average vacationer or traveler of moderate means it is hard to do anything besides move with the crowds.

Fortunately for those who prefer the pleasures of independence, there are ways to avoid, or at least minimize, having to deal with the pressures of the peripatetic tourist population. One way lies with timing; that is, planning vacation or other travel times for the off-season or shoulder seasons.

Another approach that is becoming increasingly popular in recent years, is to book a vacation rental in Europe: a cottage in the British countryside, a farm house in France, a chalet in Austria or Switzerland or a villa or apartment, perhaps in some ancient stone house in Italy, Spain, or Portugal.

Exploring Europe's *natural* waterways by renting a motor cruiser or sailing yacht, combines transportation and accommodation and provides a new perspective on how to see Europe: living aboard, and cruising the rivers and lakes of Britain and Ireland. This is not only an excellent way to get away from the crowds, but an economical one, offering independence, comfort, and fun. This is what this guidebook is about.

A Short History of the Natural Waterways

A study of a map of Europe makes clear that many of its great cities are seaports, founded and existing today precisely because they were, and remain, the touchpoints between foreign lands and other continents: Barcelona, Marseilles, Le Havre, Naples, Amsterdam, and Helsinki, to name a few. Others exist and endure because they are river ports, founded as centers of commerce along the great natural waterways of Britain, Ireland, and continental Europe: cities like Paris, Lyon, Frankfurt, Vienna, London, Zurich, Hamburg, and Cologne. And there are countless smaller cities like Stratford-upon-Avon, Oxford (on the Thames), Norwich (on the Yare and Wensum), Beccles (on the Waveney), Ireland's Carrick-on-Shannon and Enniskillen on the River Erne.

Between the cities and towns, along the banks of rivers and along the shores of lakes, there also exist the artifacts of ancient times, the manifestations of a long history. Castles and fortifications were built to guard against access by hostile armies and flotillas to the lands through which the rivers flowed; churches and abbeys were built and market towns emerged around them. Most remain along these waterways. In more recent centuries came the chateaux of France, the manor houses and stately homes of Britain, replete with gardens, many now for public view under the stewardship of Britain's National Trust. Then there are the inns, pubs, and markets that welcome travelers of the water, first established for those who were on missions of commerce (and war) and now used mostly for tourists and vacationers who travel for pleasure.

Among the first to recognize the desirability of leisure travel on the lakes and rivers of Eastern England was one Harry Blake who, in 1908, let it be known that skiffs, punts and wherries

2

(shallow-draft sailing boats) were available for hire, for the pleasure of the public, on the Norfolk and Suffolk Broads, that expansive network of rivers and lakes of East Anglia we mentioned before. Since the Broads are only a hundred miles northeast of London, many of the first boaters were Londoners who traveled by rail or coach to spend a week or a weekend on the waters. Over the years, not only have the number of boats available for rent multiplied enormously, but a support system of docks, provisioners, maintenance stations, and fuel purveyors have grown. Now there are dozens such points along the hundreds of miles of the lakeshore and the rivers of the Broads: the Ant, the Bure, the Thurne, Yare, Waveney, and Chet.

Later came the idea of outfitting barges and narrowboats for public use, to turn the commercial canals into routes for leisure travel. Many canals, long unused, began to be cleaned of decades of earth, vegetation, and rubbish, filled with water and made ready for use. So it has also been with the rivers, many of which were no longer viable for commerce, but which have instead been cleaned and tidied for the use of pleasure craft. Facilities to support and welcome pleasure boaters have been built on many of the most beautiful of these rivers and lakes, with boatyards (marinas) where cruisers can be rented by the week and subsequently supported in terms of fuel, provisions, and instruction and assistance by boatyard staff. The latest of these grand efforts was completed in late 1994 with the opening of the Ballinamore-Ballyconnell Canal that connects the upper reaches of the majestic Shannon of the Republic of Ireland with the Erne lakes of Northern Ireland, covered thoroughly in *The Natural Waterways of Ireland*, our second volume in this series.

Free-Cruising vs. Canals & Narrowboats

Free-cruising is a term we'll use to describe travel by motor cruiser or sailing yacht on open waterways. In fact, for purposes of this guidebook, the reference is to open *natural* waterways, the lakes and rivers of Britain. Free-cruising is in contrast to boating along handmade canals that cross and criss-cross these countries. The waters are different and the boats are different. What they hold in common is that the pace is leisurely, and anyone, experienced or not, can rent and operate a cabin cruiser, canal narrowboat or sailing yacht.

Some of our friends in Britain make canal boating a social event, meeting each other's narrowboats at appointed spots, often moving from pub to pub along the route. As many North Americans and Europeans know, except for sections where there are numerous locks, narrowboat travel is a relaxed, non-strenuous way of seeing a countryside often invisible to those who drive through it. There is absolutely nothing wrong with renting a narrowboat and following the courses of the many canals that criss-cross Britain, especially England and Wales. The narrowboats are quaint yet reasonably comfortable, restricted only by their narrow beams. The drawbacks are that the course of the canals must be followed and the locks themselves can often require physical effort; faster-paced boats may press from behind or a line of slow boats in front cause waits and delays. And, in inclement weather there is little relief for the crew member who must remain in the rain to handle the tiller.

For natural-water cruising, many motor cruiser designs are of broader beam, and they offer a variety of configurations ranging from the familiar design we see in marinas around the United States and Canada, to the single level slide-top cruisers popular in the Norfolk Broads of eastern England. Itineraries, directions, and mooring spots are open to choice, especially on the Broads and on Scotland's chain of Highland lakes. On the clear-water Thames from west London into Gloucestershire the choice of cruising style is quite open and the traffic is fairly light. The only handmade canal in the guide is the short one that connects Loch Ness, Loch Oich, and Loch Lochy in Scotland, a minor part of the waterway. In a nutshell, free-cruising differs from canal boating by providing freedom to go where you want and when you want and to go at your own pace (so long as it's slow) and to moor where you please. It's a matter of independence. Whether your interest is in wildlife, history, pubs and inns, exploring waterside towns and cities, or simply boating—or all of these—this is an ideal and economical way for families and friends, as well as for couples, to travel and explore.

Again, because self-skippered rental cruisers and sailing yachts are not common in North America, we emphasize that these boats are not canal narrowboats. They are comfortable vessels that are free to move wherever you wish because you, the renter, are the planner of your itinerary and control the helm. The motor cruisers can be rented and handled by most anyone, even novices who have never operated a boat of any kind before. Novices renting sailing yachts need more instruction time, but even this is handled easily and quickly and the instruction is free. All the vessels are built for ease of handling, maneuverability and comfort rather than speed, and provide the ultimate way for exploring the waters and the countryside, combining a place to live with a means of travel.

The Purpose of this Guide
When considering any new adventure, the difficulty for most travelers—beginners and experienced alike—is how to decide where to spend a week or more on the journey. There are six regions covered in the guide. Five are in England and one in Scotland, all of which lend themselves to extensive exploration by boat. Some are well defined: the string of Highland lakes, the River Thames. Others, including the Norfolk Broads and the six rivers that flow through them are so expansive that they cannot be thoroughly explored in the span of an average vacation or foreign visit. But a week or two is ample, leaving some waters and adventures for another time.

This book will help travelers plan their trips by describing the features of each of the areas: their geographic and topographic nature, an overview of their wildlife and flora, their historical character in terms of towns and villages, abbeys, castles, and the like, as well as the waters themselves. The variety of itineraries and the best times to go will help in planning and, finally, we provide a short overview of the hospitality of the region to boaters in terms of waterside pubs, grocers, fuel and other support, and general access to places of interest.

We also introduce the companies and the boats. For seasoned sailor and beginner alike, we provide the details of how to obtain information, how to choose among the many types and sizes of cruisers and sailing yachts, and how to decipher the rental agreements, insurance terms, and damage deposits. Each chapter will provide an overview of the boats available in the region, what charts are important and how to obtain them, and how to book and pay for the rental. The guide will explain how the short introduction to boating and training takes place and how these differ between motor cruisers and sailboats. Support services on the waterways are noted, along with particular boatyards and boats that seem best for travelers from abroad.

To many Britons, renting a boat for a week on the waters is no more unusual than renting a car. For most North Americans, however, not only is the whole idea of such water exploration new, but the process of making wise choices and arranging the booking from this side of the Atlantic may seem daunting. It is not, and this guide is designed to make it both understandable and achievable.

Almost anyone can take the helm. *Experience not required!* You must be over eighteen years of age and in reasonably good health (sixteen when accompanied by an adult). Except in the sea off Scotland's west coast, there are no restrictions regarding experience. For persons with no boating experience, the staff of the rental company will provide a hands-on training session at the time of boat pickup.

To Novices and Newcomers

There is nothing about the operation and navigation of the rental motor cruisers that cannot be learned from scratch in an hour or so. A staff person at the boatyard will spend enough time training the renter in a hands-on session to assure that the boat can be handled properly and safely. It is, after all, in the owners' interest to make sure that their $30,000 to $250,000 investments don't wind up in somebody's yard or athwart a pier piling.

The charts provided by the boat renters are very detailed, and interpreting them is self-evident. Markers on the charts are accurately keyed to the navigation symbols posted in the various waterways, so it's easy to know precisely where you are at all times. Only once did we go astray, misreading our chart and turning too soon into what we thought was a broad channel between islands in Ireland's Loch Erne. It was instead a shallow bay and we soon ran aground. We lightened the boat by one of us getting into the dinghy with our heaviest luggage and the groceries. It worked—we eased our way out. Despite our success, as we cleared the bay we saw a boat heading toward us, obviously coming to help. When they saw we were free they came about and returned to the marina.

There is always someone to lend a hand. Rangers keep an eye in the Norfolk Broads and discretely patrol the Thames. Staff at commercial rental boatyards are always alert to any problems in their vicinity.

The sailing yachts and motor-sailors on the Broads, Highland lakes and Lake Windermere are somewhat more complicated, requiring a little more initial instruction and more attention during the span of the rental period. But as noted earlier, the instruction is offered at no cost to beginners. As one company puts it: *No sailing experience? Don't worry. A two to four hour trip with an experienced yachtsman from the boatyard teaches you ample to set off on your own with complete confidence. Hundreds of absolute beginners have learned to sail with us over the last few years.*

The waters that the rental cruisers travel are calm; the atmosphere that prevails among boaters is that of relaxation. People are going places at a slow speed; there is much stopping, bird watching, photographing, identifying shore plants, tying up to walk a waterside path or explore a ruin. Pauses at waterside pubs or inns, at docks in quaint market villages, at parks, at castles and the ruins of monastic communities pleasantly absorb all the time that isn't spent cruising, eating and sleeping. There are no races or high speed runs; roaring engines are not allowed. Boating of this kind in Britain and Ireland is seen as a civilized pastime, a means of experiencing places otherwise inaccessible, traveling quietly through natural habitat. With a week to travel perhaps a hundred and twenty miles, there is no rush. Even beginners will feel quite relaxed (as well as delighted) by the end of the first day out.

The Training: A Summary of Instruction

Even experienced operators will be introduced to the boating area, charts and chart reading, safety procedures, and the mechanics of the cruiser (or sailing yacht), and will be taken out for a short operational overview. For novices, the training will be somewhat longer and instructions of a more basic nature will be included, such as:

- Assignment of tasks for the crew. Even if there are only two people, both must be able to take the helm and both must understand the deck and dock work necessary to moor, cast off, and handle any locks that may be encountered.

- Starting the cruiser and the operation of the throttle and gearbox (most cruisers have only a one handle combined throttle and gearbox for forward and reverse).

- Reading the simple gauges: what they mean and what to do should they indicate a problem.

- Knots: how to tie the proper hitch (there are really only two to memorize) so that the boat can be securely tied to the bollard, cleat, or ring, or any waterside post or tree, for that matter.

- Lines: mooring lines pass UNDER any on-boat rails when mooring.

- Mooring: You'll learn steering, speed and direction control for mooring, and will understand the importance of approaching moorings with the boat headed upstream. This gives maximum steering control and enables you to bring the boat to a very slow speed, or even a dead stop when the upriver speed of the boat equals the speed of the current. Our first instructor observed that when your boat isn't moving, it's hard to incur any damage. If you approach the dock, wharf or pier at less than a mile-per-hour, it's easy for the person with the deck assignment to step ashore and tie up. If you are headed downstream, simply pass by the mooring point, make a U-turn and approach with the bow pointed upstream.

In addition to the video and the hands-on instruction, each "Captain's Handbook" contains point-by-point details on everything from checking-in to CPR and what to do if you run aground. Remember: *you are never alone.* There are always other boaters to lend a hand, always a ranger or a boatyard staff member keeping an eye out. The only time we ran aground, we sat unmoving, knowing we were stuck in the muddy bottom. We thought about raising the distress flag, and having a sandwich while we pondered our situation. Instead we loaded our luggage and some groceries and one of us into the dinghy, felt ourselves float free, and we headed for deep water. Nevertheless, it was nice to see the cruiser from the marina coming and to know that someone had been watching.

Although there is not much physical effort required, there are nonetheless activities which demand attention and a modicum of work. Locks are the cause for most of the labor, and although there are far, far fewer than those encountered by narrowboats on the canals, they do exist on some of the rivers, on the canals that may be included as part of a multi-river itinerary, and between lakes such as those in Scotland that form part of the Caledonian Canal. The operation of locks is not difficult and will be described later in the book. They will also be explained by boatyard staff before your departure.

There is also the task of carrying groceries aboard, making berths and doing "household" chores. Like any boats, most do not lend themselves well to persons with serious visual impairments or walking disabilities. But if you are concerned, discuss with the rental company which boats are the best for disabled persons.

We do not want to minimize the fact that in some areas a little effort is needed, but the leisurely pace doesn't call for heroic effort. Not long ago we met a man who extolled the pleasures of a Thames River journey. Having been to England before, they had decided that a week would do. They wanted plenty of space, so they selected a cruiser that would sleep six (and were pleasantly surprised by the modest price). Neither he nor his wife had ever operated a motor vessel before and were a bit tentative, especially because he was seventy-two, his wife of similar age, and they were taking her mother on the trip. So great was their pleasure that they extended their journey to two weeks and traveled the Thames from London westward, beyond their original plan of ending at Abingdon, all the way to the end of the line at Lechlade, Gloucestershire and returned.

Boat Rental Companies & their Agents
There are dozens of boatyards scattered along the waterways of England, Scotland, and Wales. They are independent companies that own fleets of motor cruisers and/or sailing

yachts to rent. They are the outfitters of the waterways, providing fuel, charts, supplies, training sessions for beginners, support, and emergency response, as well as the boats themselves. There is Eastwood Whelpton on the River Bure, Neatishead Boatyard and Rivercraft on the Ant. York Marine is on the River Ouse in Yorkshire, Maidline and Kris are on the Thames; Caley is at Inverness and Windermere Holidays Afloat is at home in Bowness. There are many more dotted along the many hundreds of miles of lakeshores and river banks of Britain's and Ireland's waterways.

All of these independent boat companies and boatyards are vying with each other for clients, and each has its own descriptive brochures, website, contracts and terms and conditions, and each its own booking procedures and price lists and mechanisms for payment. Consolidating all this from abroad, gathering all the information needed to make the right choices and the final arrangements, can be difficult. We recommend instead, a few companies with fleets in several locations and a handful of major organizations that serve as agents, or brokers, representing many of the boat renting companies. In Britain, for example, Blakes Holidays Ltd. of Hoveton (Wroxham) and Hoseasons Holidays Ltd. of Lowestoft serve as the marketers for the many boatyards on many waterways. They compete, and there is no duplication of representation. That is, Blakes has their members and Hoseasons has theirs. Both companies have "member" fleets that compete in some of the same areas such as the Broads, the Thames, and the Scottish lakes, while others are exclusive. It's a matter of geography: finding navigable rivers and lakes and being the first to establish a boatyard there. There is a Blakes-associated boat company on Yorkshire's Ouse, for example, while Hoseasons has none, although both have canal narrowboats in this region. Independent operations on smaller waters such as beautiful Lake Windermere in Cumbria, have recently joined the Blakes listing.

The decision on whether to book directly with the rental boat company, or with Blakes or Hoseasons, or with a US agent, depends in part on how much time and effort you want to put into the search, and whether or not you want to talk with someone in the States who can make recommendations that will best suit your needs. The easiest ways to gather information on specific boats and their cost are to obtain copies of the enticing and wonderfully descriptive color catalogs and check websites. Catalogs especially cover every waterway and describe and picture a vast array of types, sizes and quality standards of boat. It also means that rather than dealing with dozens of boatyards there are a few single sources for obtaining information and, finally, one company to book through and to pay (credit cards accepted). This makes the process very easy. Each of our regional chapters contains information on how to obtain the catalog. And much of this information is also now available on the internet.

Each boatyard seems to offer particular styles and classes within their fleet, and many have a descriptive brochure for the asking, so just contact them. Carefully look over the cruiser or sailboat descriptions in the Blakes or Hoseasons catalogs or cruiser company brochures. Feel free to telephone either the agents or, if you want to discuss specifics about a particular boat, area, itinerary, provisioning, transportation to the boatyard and the like, telephone the boatyard directly. A phone conversation is often well worth the small cost.

Select several suitable vessels that appeal to your needs and taste and suit your budget. Concentrate on the fleets of the boatyards that are most conveniently reached, especially if you will be arriving by rail or bus. The prices for all vessels at all seasonal periods are included with the catalog and/or on the websites. Choose at least two boat styles in low season and three or four in summer, and either list them on the booking form in the catalog and send it by air mail, or fax the booking form. If you have a computer, bookings can also be made by e-mail or via their web page.

Again, we recommend at least one telephone call to discuss with the agent or boat company any details that are not clear. Tell them about your family or party: ages, children, gender, experienced or beginner, whether you want to concentrate on operating a large and complex boat, or prefer an easy one on which to sightsee and relax. They know the vessels and will give good advice. If you have never sailed or have never operated a motor cruiser before, be sure to mention this and confirm the day and time that the instruction session will take place. For cruisers, this is done on the start day during the hours before departing on your own. For sailing instruction, this may vary. All of this will be made clear in the instructions you will receive after booking, but you should feel free to telephone if you are in doubt about any details.

Contacting the boat company directly has the advantage of being able to communicate with someone on the scene: a person who intimately knows their cruisers, the boatyard, the surroundings, and the waterway. Most of the companies have brochures with cruiser photographs and layouts as well as the price list, and many have their own website. A phone conversation with boatyard proprietors or staff will likely be helpful whether you book directly with them or through a US or British agent. We feel this is especially true with cruiser companies on the Shannon-Erne Waterway.

Prices are the same whether booking directly with the boat rental company or through Blakes or Hoseasons. Commission arrangements are internal business between the boat companies and the agents and do not affect the consumer. The only price difference may be when booking with one of the US agents, so compare the prices. Both Blakes and Hoseasons have agents in the US. The US-based agents listed should have had experience traveling the various regions and should offer ideas and suggestions, as well as have websites and make catalogs and brochures available more quickly than waiting for delivery from overseas. These agents must of course cover their costs of domestic advertising, telephone, processing of the financial dealings with the boat companies and the like, so expect to pay a slight commission for these services rendered. How much? Ask them. (We think up to ten percent is reasonable, for the personal service and for dealing with the daily US dollar to £ sterling fluctuations—or even just for the peace of mind from dealing "locally.") You will incur no telephone or fax charges as with booking directly overseas. In the case of agent Jody Lexow Yacht Charters there is no add-on commission, but a $100 flat fee. US Agent Blakes Vacations includes its US $ price list, so check it against the current dollar to £ sterling exchange.

Take care if you book through a regular travel agency, as the price might be even higher. Very few regular travel agents have personal knowledge about specific waterways, boatyards and boats, and many of them simply arrange bookings through one of the North American boat rental agencies.

When planning the overseas flights, take into account that many rental periods run Saturday to Saturday, but if this is impossible or is in conflict with the best flight schedules or fares, discuss other starting days. There is considerable flexibility during the low and shoulder seasons when there are idle cruisers. Further, as mentioned before, we recommend arriving in the vicinity of the boatyard a day or more before the start day in order to have a fresh start for cruising.

We recommend using a credit card for payment (all the companies accept at least Visa and MasterCard). When the company receives the booking form it will confirm the boat and the dates. Generally, if the booking is made more than eight weeks in advance of your dates, the company will charge your account with a deposit fee of about 25% of the total rental price; the amount is dependent on the size of the boat rented and is shown in £ sterling in the catalog. If the booking is made eight weeks or less in advance, the full rental will be charged.

The booking will then be confirmed by mail, e-mail or fax. If you are working well in advance and only the deposit has been charged, do not forget to telephone, e-mail or fax again at least four weeks in advance with authorization to charge your account for the balance. The alternative is to handle payment by sending bank drafts in £ sterling or by wire transfer (information on this is in the catalogs). If you prefer to make the selection and booking by telephone, be sure to have your boat selections identified by their reference numbers.

British Agents

- Blakes Holidays Ltd.
  Wroxham, Norfolk NR12 8DH, England
  Tel: 1603-739400
  Fax: 1603-782871
  E-mail: boats@blakes.co.uk
  Website: www.blakes.co.uk

- Hoseasons Holidays Ltd.
  Lowestoft, Suffolk NR32 3LT, England
  Tel: 1502-501010
  Fax: 1502-586781
  E-mail: mail@hoseasons.co.uk
  Website: www.hoseasons.co.uk

US Agents

For Blakes:
- Great Trips Unlimited, Portland, Oregon
  Tel: 888-329-9720
  Fax: 503-297-5308
  E-mail: admin@gtunlimited.com
  Website: www.gtunlimited.com
  Blakes Vacations, Skokie, Illinois
  Tel: 800-628-8118
  Fax: 847-244-8118

E-mail: blakes1076@aol.com
Website: www. blakesvacations.com

For Hoseasons and Connoisseur:
• Jody Lexow Yacht Charters, Newport, Rhode Island
Tel: 800-662-2628
Fax: 401-845-8909
E-mail: jlyc@edgenet.com
Website: www.jodylexowyachtcharters.com

For Connoisseur Cruisers:
• Le Boat, Maywood, New Jersey
Tel: 800-922-0291
E-mail: leboatinc@worldnet.att.net
Website: www.leboat.com

For Silver Line Cruisers:
• Isle Inn Tours
Tel: 800-237-9376; 703-683-4800
Fax: 703-683-4812
E-mail: isleinn@msn.com
Website: www.isleinntours.com

For New Horizons Holidays:
• Great Trips Unlimited
Tel: 888-329-9720
Website: www.gtunlimited.com

The government tourist offices of Britain, Northern Ireland, and the Republic of Ireland also all have unbiased information on boat rental companies and boating. From these publications the companies can be contacted directly. Also, readers with internet access can obtain contact information from several sources:
Marine Internet: www.marineinternet.com/directory

Inland Waterway Association:
www.man.ac.uk/cme/iwa/iwahome

In addition to the rental companies and the agents, there are also non-profit associations that serve as clearing houses for rentals of members' boats. Most prominent are The Association of Pleasure Craft Operators and The Thames Hire Cruiser Association. The role played by these various companies, agencies, and associations in terms of how they affect decisions, costs, and booking from overseas is explained in each chapter dealing with the regions. They are not hard to sort out, but the key is finding the best way to work directly with someone who knows about boats and the waterways.

The Motor Cruisers

The introduction and training for motor cruisers takes from one to two hours, depending on whether you are experienced or not. Step one in many cases is a general video about boat operation, navigation, chart reading, and safety; if the company doesn't have a video, a staff person explains it all. This is followed by hands-on instruction by a staff member, the duration will depend on your experience (or lack of it). The first part is normally a matter of about half an hour, and includes instruction on everything from how to operate the showers and hob (the stove), to how to remove and empty the weed filter, check the oil, operate the lights and TV, and read the instruments. With the instructor, you then push off and spend an hour or so cruising near the boatyard, learning to steer, to handle the throttle and gear box, to read the charts and, most important, how to come alongside a quay, pier, or jetty and tie up.

The cruisers are not complex to operate. The throttle and gears, for example, are normally combined in one handle: from neutral, push forward to go forward, push more forward to go faster. Pull back to stop, farther back to reverse, even farther back to go faster in reverse. We recommend cabin cruisers over sailing yachts for anyone with little or no experience who wants to concentrate on the surroundings rather than on boat operation.

The variety of motor cruisers available for rent is astonishing. Among the motor vessels in Britain and Ireland the basic configurations are the aft-cockpit cruiser, the center-cockpit cruiser, the forward-drive cruiser, and the Flybridge style cruiser. These come in all configurations and sizes, some with a sliding roof, some with a sliding canopy, some with glass doors to the sundeck, some with one full bathroom (with shower), others with two, some with separate showers, others with two toilet rooms and a separate shower and so forth. The smallest sleep two and are about twenty-six feet in length, with a nine-foot beam. The largest sleep ten and boast five separate cabins, two showers, three toilets, a forty-eight-foot length and a twelve-plus foot beam. There is practically every size, combination, and configuration in-between. All have complete, fully-equipped galleys, as well as all kitchenware and dinnerware needed to match the needs of the number of people on board. Most include color TV, but on some this is provided for a small extra fee.

In the catalogs, and some websites, photographs of each boat are accompanied by written descriptions and diagrams of the boat layout. They show the relative size and the placement of all the cabins, galley, salon, cockpit, head (WC), cubbies and usually even the placement of the cabinets, refrigerator, tables, and berths.

Each chapter will make clear the variety of boats available in that specific region, as well as the companies that rent them. The process of deciding which company to deal with and which boat to rent is quite straightforward. There are three questions to be answered: (1) Which region or waterway? (2) How many in your party? (3) What is your budget? The descriptions of the regions and waterways in the later chapters of this book may help you answer the first two questions.

The Search for a European Getaway

Although it depends somewhat on configuration, as a basic rule we recommend renting a boat rated to sleep more than will actually be cruising together. The price difference to step up one notch is relatively small and, we feel, well worth it. Also, consider a larger boat if you are planning to go for more than one week. Couples cruising for a week, for example, should rent a boat that sleeps three to four, ideally at least a twenty-nine-by-ten-foot craft. A couple with a child will also do well in this size cruiser if there is not too much luggage.

With a few exceptions, most boat companies stretch the number of persons their boats can accommodate. This isn't intentional, but not being used to boaters from across the Atlantic they rarely think about space for extra luggage and clothing. They are also used to travelers from the Continent, some of whom have cars, and many of whom don't seem to be as accustomed to extra space as are Americans and Canadians. Whatever the reason, don't simply take the figures for the number of berths as the defining factor for your boat selection. Look at layout, look at beam as well as length, and consider well the composition of your family or group. In sum, the key to selection is to study the configurations in the brochures or the website, mentally place each crew member in a berth, look for space for luggage (spare berth or spare cabin), and determine the crew's need for toilets and showers. Look at the photos as well as the diagrams for outside deck space in which to have morning coffee, lunch, or to fish from or soak up the sun. Look, too, for a covering or canopy extending over the aft deck, where it's possible to stand protected from rain; also for inner space—imagine cruising in the rain.

Next is to look at the price list; find the price band or price code for the maximum of your budget for the time of year you want to rent. Again, remember that other than the first and possibly last nights, no accommodations or rental cars will be required. Finally, peruse the catalog, marking the vessels that look good to you, accommodate the number in your group, and show a price band number equal to or less than the number you have budgeted for. From these boats, pick and rank several that have the configuration and general appearance which most appeal to you, and let the company know of your decision by phone, fax or e-mail. They will then let you know which are available at the specified time.

Comments on special regional designs as well recommendations for selections best suited for the various waterways will be found in the appropriate chapters on the individual waterways.

The Sailing Yachts

We do not deal in depth with sailing yachts in this guide because we don't want to shift the focus away from the environment toward the learning and practice of sailing itself as a sport. Also, as many of our readers will be, we are relative newcomers to motor cruising and are far from being experienced sailors. What we learned about boating we learned from the lessons given by boatyard operators in Ireland and Britain, just as any novice might. Real sailors might scoff at the minimal training for operating sailing vessels, but the purpose is to let novices enjoy the sport while not harming themselves or others. We do not want to diminish the potential for learning to sail, nor to discourage experienced sailors from enjoying the waters of Britain. They can be made as taxing as you want them to be. Try tacking up the Waveney where the tree-lined banks are only fifty feet apart.

Although the motor vessels are available from boatyards in many parts of Britain, the sailing yachts are rented only on the waterways of the Norfolk Broads, Lake Windermere in Cumbria, and on the Scottish Highland lakes. They need the expanses that even rivers like the clearwater Thames rarely offer, although skilled sailors can handle the rivers of the Broads, such as the Waveney, Yare and Bure.

The sailboats, or sailing yachts as they are usually referred to in Britain, are available to novice as well as experienced sailors, although only after completing at least three hours and often a full half-day of training, conducted by an experienced sailor on the boatyard staff. The idea that learning to sail is a complex task that takes much time and practice is put to rest by learning to sail in one of the "hire" yachts on the Norfolk Broads, the Scottish lakes, or Windermere. This is not to say that after a few hours one will become an expert sailor, but it is certainly possible to become one who is adequate, can keep out of trouble, and can avoid encounters with other boats. The key for the novice is to pick the simplest yacht to operate in terms of its hull design and, most important, its rigging.

As with the motor cruisers, there is an array of configurations, sizes and quality standards among the sailboats. Most, however, are designed for use by beginners as well as experienced sailors in that the rigging is as simple and straightforward as possible. The assumption in their design is that they will be used by persons possessing minimal sailing skills. They are also designed for the waters in which they will be used. Nevertheless, tacking up the River Waveney or the Yare can call forth the skills of seasoned sailors. All are equipped with an auxiliary engine, usually a small diesel, and like the motor vessels, come with full galley, all kitchenware, dinnerware, and linens.

Typically, the sailing yachts range in length from twenty-seven to thirty-four feet, with six- to ten-foot beams, and sleep from two to six persons. The largest is an elegant fifty-nine-foot Wherry Yacht on the Broads; it sleeps six to ten persons. (But this is a singular vessel, the only one that must be rented with a skipper, who has separate quarters and will sail the boat as much or as little as the renter wishes.)

The simplest sail rigging of all, and well suited for the beginner, is known as an "una rig," a one-sail affair that reduces sail work to a minimum. Technically, yachts with two sails are known as sloops, and sloops encompass ninety percent of the hire yachts available. Among sloops are several riggings, the most popular being the Bermuda sloop, graceful, easy to operate (only one halyard to hoist the sail), and fun to sail. These are predominant among rental yachts.

Anyone who has never skippered a sailing yacht should defer to the boatyard operator to select the proper yacht— they know their boats. There is a good choice of sizes (sleeping from two to eight), so the limiting factor for novices is the simplicity. Also, catalogs note when particular boats should be avoided by novices.

Typically, two to three hours of sailing instruction are offered at no cost, with extra hours available for a fee. And remember, all the rental yachts are basically "motor-sailors," so at any time the sails can come down and you can cruise to the rhythm of the engine.

Several of the boatyards specialize in classic wood hull sailing yachts, boats built early this century, rich in history, fine woods and brass.

Rental Prices and Overall Costs

The specifics are contained in each of the appropriate area chapters, but rental prices range in the neighborhood of the cost of a vacation apartment in London or Dublin, and well below that of city hotel rooms of equal standards. Just as prices for hotel rooms, apartments, and other accommodations, boat prices are dependent on two factors: size and quality standards. The size factor is self-explanatory, and the standard has to do with the quality of the boat fittings, decor, furnishings, spaciousness and, sometimes, age of the vessel. One company assigns ratings: standard, 3-star, 4-star and blue chip. It is also easy to scan the catalogs and compare the size, layout and appearance of the various boats with the price band or price group number always shown with the description. The fact is: you get what you pay for. If two boats are of the same size, same type and similar appearance, yet one rents for $500 per week and the other for $700 per week in the same season, the latter will usually be the most comfortable, convenient and of a higher standard, whether it is rated superior or not. With so many boatyards, the prices set must be competitive and agreed upon between the boatyard and the agent, or the boatyard will suffer.

The range of prices, like the standards, is considerable, from economy to high. Nevertheless, we have been consistently impressed by the comparatively modest prices and excellent value for these vessels. For example: The price of a room for two at London's Hyatt Carlton Tower, the Grosvenor, the Savoy and the Sheraton Park Tower averages £1,650 (about US $2,650) per week. The most expensive motor cruiser on the Thames, a forty-eight-foot luxury vessel that accommodates ten persons in five separate cabins, rents for £1,275 (about $2,040) per week in the peak months of July and August, and $1,500 in June and September (and lower yet in the off-season). Typical B&B rooms in Britain run in the neighborhood of $60 or more per night ($420 per week); a pleasant twenty-six-foot cruiser for two can be rented for between $385 and $600 per week, depending on the season. Even though the price of the smaller cruiser is modest, it can be seen that the larger the vessel, the lower the cost per person.

Fuel is extra, but we were surprised to learn that a combination of engine efficiency, hull design and the relatively slow pace of cruising on most of these waters keeps the cost quite low. Diesel costs will run between £3 and £6 per day (US $30 to $60 per week), depending on the size of the vessel and the speed at which it is operated.

Remember that the boat is both the vehicle and the accommodation, as well as the place for breakfast and any other meals "in." Required cancellation and holiday insurance will run about $50, but insurance on the boat is included in the price. If you drive to the boatyard and leave the car, the cost will range from nothing to $20 for parking (there is more information on getting to the boatyards in each of the regional chapters).

In sum, a family of four with modest requirements, or two couples sharing, can enjoy a week in a spacious motor cruiser with two sleeping cabins for under US $1,000, during the two peak summer months, $750 in June and September and $600 in other months, with everything included except food and beverage. Add roughly $100 per week for the same size vessel but of luxury standard. A final cost to figure in is the price for at least a few meals ashore. For most travelers, the inviting nature of many of the waterside pubs and inns is too compelling to resist.

Sailing yacht rental prices also cover a wide range, but the boats themselves should not be compared to motor cruisers in terms of dimensions or cabin space; their design is completely different; space is exchanged for the fun of sailing. Nevertheless, prices are also remarkably modest. The least expensive is typically a twenty-one to twenty-four foot sloop with berths for two persons; the berths are usually what is referred to as settee berths, that is, single beds made from the convertible settees on the main cabin. A fully-equipped boat of this type rents from $450 per week during the period from mid-September to mid-June (with a few national and bank holiday exceptions) to about $500 in the high season months. A lovely thirty-foot top of the line sloop that sleeps six (for the more experienced sailor) rents from about $850 to $1,050 per week, depending on the season. To these prices should be added $20 or so for fuel for the auxiliary motor and the $50 insurance fee noted above.

Mooring fees vary, but most of them are free at any of the many boatyards and marinas associated with each particular boat rental company. Fees at public moorings are also either free or cost very little, and even private moorings are still quite inexpensive, running in the neighborhood of a few pounds per day.

Basic Planning

Planning your waterways adventure is dependent on which of the boating areas are of most interest. Each of the regional waterways chapters in this guide provides information on the physical character of the area and the boat rental system, adequate to help you make the best decisions and arrange the most rewarding journey. Each region requires some variation on the basic procedure of gathering boat rental company information, selecting your cruiser or sailing yacht, determining the availability on the dates you want and, finally, booking and paying. But there is one early decision common to all: TIMING.

The rental period set by most boatyards is Saturday to Saturday. For travelers from overseas, this is not always the best day of the week in terms of trans-Atlantic flights and fares, nor is it always the most convenient for vacationers who must take their time according to company calendars and schedules. Of the several steps which can be taken to overcome this potential problem, the first is to try to avoid going in July or August, the months when most boatyards adhere quite rigidly to the Saturday start dates. During the rest of the year there is much more flexibility, beginning with a choice of Saturday or Sunday start days. During the months when there are fewer boaters, mid-week starts and shorter rental periods, normally three-day minimums, are available. This varies between boatyards, so select three or four suitable vessels and either fax, e-mail or telephone the rental company stipulating the dates you want. This will work in the off-seasons, usually including the pleasant boating months of May, early June and much of September.

If you are planning your trip for the period between mid-June and the first week of September, the months during which air fares as well as boat prices are highest, the best approach is to first arrange the best flight and best fare, then set your cruising period dates. Plan to arrive in Britain a few days early, then take a hotel or B&B in the area of your selected boatyard. This makes your trip to the boatyard leisurely, allows time to get over jet-lag, makes the Saturday start day feasible, and may save you money on the air fare.

Transportation

We rarely recommend one airline over another, but when the service and comfort provided is exceptional we feel that there should be acknowledgement. Flights with Britain's Virgin Atlantic Airlines and British Airways have been top notch.

Serving the UK (London Heathrow & Gatwick unless noted otherwise)
> Virgin Atlantic Airlines Tel: 800-862-8621;
> www.fly.virgin.com/atlantic
> British Airways Tel: 800-247-9297l;
> www.british-airways.com;
> United Airlines Tel: 800-241-6522; www.ual.com
> TWA Tel: 800-221-2000; www.twa.com (Gatwick only)
> Delta Airlines Tel: 800-221-1212; www.delta-air.com
> Continental Airlines Tel: 800-231-0856;
> www.flycontinental.com (Gatwick)

For railway schedules from your destination city to the boatyards, purchase a *Thomas Cook European Timetables* or, for information and booking contact:
> *Rail Pass Express*
> Point-to-point ticket information: Tel: 614-793-7650
> (9:00 AM–3:00 PM EST M-F); www.railpass.com; e-mail:
> relations@railpass.com
> For rail passes & point-to-point tickets: Tel: 800-722-7151
> Simply tell the agent your departure point and destination town, and your itinerary will be set: for example, from London's Liverpool Street Station, to an intervening station in Ipswich or Norwich, to the Broads town where your boat

awaits you. Passes, rather than point-to-point tickets, are appropriate for travelers planning rail excursions before or after cruising. Payment can be made by credit card. As they will be mailed, buy tickets at least three weeks in advance.

Navigational Charts, Guides, & Environmental Information

Waterways are as scrupulously charted as any road map, and the charts are as easy to follow, perhaps more so because they are less complex. Moreover, the charts are often combined with detailed guides that provide not only full navigational information but locations and descriptions of all the boatyards in the area, small maps of the town and other moorings, waterside inns, restaurants, pubs, footpaths, roads from the water's edge, special attractions. Anything a boat traveler may need is included. These waterways have been plied for centuries, and many of them for pleasure alone for over a hundred years. A water-focused world exists and continues to grow, and there are many regional publications aimed at helping the traveler get the most enjoyment from it. Site-specific charts and guides, with titles such as "Nicholson's New Ordinance Survey Map to the River Thames," or "Pubs of the Norfolk Broads," can be purchased from the boat rental agencies and from most individual boatyards. Once you have decided the waterway you want to travel, we suggest ordering the appropriate local guide from the list in the rentals catalog. They are fun and informative to peruse.

Specific books on the flora and fauna of the regions are also available, some available through the boat rental companies, but many can be found in libraries and bookstores in the United States. We especially enjoyed having a good bird book along.

Waterside Support

Boatyards, or boatbases, can be likened to a combination of a land-based service station and car rental office. On the Thames, for example, one rental organization lists several associated boatyards along the 125-mile (205 km) stretch of navigable river from London west into Gloucestershire (see map in Chapter 3). All are easy to reach by land as well as by water, enabling travelers to pick up and drop their boats at their convenience. For North Americans arriving at Heathrow, for example, there are three rental boatyards on the Thames within fifteen miles of the airport. Because many travelers from overseas may not choose to rent a car, each chapter of the guide contains recommendations and profiles on the best and most convenient pickup and drop-off boatyards accessible by rail, bus, mini-bus and taxi.

The motor cruisers, houseboats and sailing yachts are always checked out, clean, fueled and ready to go. Each "Captain's Handbook" contains complete information on what to do in case of emergency or for any need of assistance such as non-emergency failure of the refrigerator, cabin heater, TV, engine and the like. Every member of the hire boat associations in Britain and Ireland is pledged to assist any boater in trouble, thus creating a network of boater support throughout the waterways systems. Telephone numbers are provided in order to call the boatyard; distress flags are provided, to be flown so that any boater will come to your aid.

Provisioning: The Essentials

Provisioning is like shopping anywhere. Before departure it is simply a matter of going to the nearest grocery store to buy food and other basics for a couple of days. Because it varies among the boat companies, ask at the rental office about what supplies, if any, are provided. For coffee drinkers, the item we most often found missing was a coffee maker or even cone-type filter. And we rarely found those most useful supplies such as liquid soap, salt, pepper, sugar, paper towels, paper napkins, zip-closure bags and hand soap. If not already aboard, buy what is needed, including (for coffee drinkers) a small plastic filter cone holder, or one of the neat collapsible net filters that we have found only in the UK and Ireland.

There are refrigerators on all the boats, but the freezers are usually small. There is no need to buy food for the week because it's easy (by following the site specific charts) to tie up at some town quay along the water and do the shopping in the village. We leaned, as we don't at home, toward prepared foods, of which British markets, even the small 24-hour type such as SPAR (like the U.S. 7-Eleven) offer an abundance, ranging from all sorts of pot pies, meat and vegetable pasties, quiches, curries, deli salads and, of course, pizzas. Many small grocery stores thrive on cruising clientele so there is no absence of any kind of food, unless you crave Mexican.

Most boat companies send with the booking form a grocery shopping list that can be ordered ahead and delivered to your boat on the day of arrival. If there is no list and you want to order in advance, just ask the boat company if they will place an order, then draw up a list and send it. There is rarely a delivery fee—the order is simply placed with the nearby local grocer who does the shopping for you and takes it to the boatyard. It's a good way to start, even if it's just for the basic supplies mentioned above plus coffee, tea, milk, bread, breakfast items, fruit and perhaps something frozen for the first night out.

Rent-a-Dinghy & Rent-a-Bicycle

Two types of small auxiliary boats are available for rent: rowing dinghies and sailing dinghies. If you are renting a motor cruiser or one of the larger sailboats, it is a good idea to rent a rowing dinghy (at about $60 per week), for the added convenience. In

Ireland, most boat rentals come with dinghy included. But for fun as well as convenience, especially if you are taking a motor vessel, but would like to play around with sailing, rent a sailing dinghy (about $75). In addition to the sport of it, there are times when one of these small boats comes in handy, such as for fishing, for venturing for a short distance into a canal or small estuary where your larger boat cannot sail, or for going ashore from your boat if it is anchored or tied up away from the dock.

Bicycles are also available for rent, or can be arranged for, at most boatyards, and taken on board. They are modestly priced and enable travelers to explore the waterside paths, fens and forests as well as make greater distances through towns.

The Boat and Cottage Option

In the preface we described our first contact with the world of rental boats, describing our stay in a modern townhouse facing a strip of grass and a row of small trees bordering a concrete quay. In fact, the townhouse we were renting was one of literally hundreds of "cottages" available throughout Great Britain for short term vacation rent from Blakes, the same company that rents the boats. Although it is no longer in the cottage rental business, the other large boat rental company, Hoseasons, remains a cottage rental organization.

We have long been champions of settling in for a week or two when visiting Europe. Staying in a vacation rental—whether it is an apartment in London or Venice, a farmhouse in Provence, or a chalet in the Alps—immerses one in the local culture, and not only provides more space and lower cost, but a sense of being part of the community rather than just a tourist. This approach to visiting Europe seems to combine nicely with the idea of renting a boat. A week exploring by waterway coupled with a week or so in a rental cottage or villa or apartment is ideal. Renting a land-bound accommodation is as easy as renting a boat, with much of the same planning devoted to choosing a location.

There are *always* cottage rentals available in the vicinity of the waterways covered in this guide: The Moretons and Sudeley Castle Cottages near Tewekesbury, Rural Retreats in the north Cotswolds near the Avon, Ecosse Unique Limited near the Highland lakes, among many others. In each chapter information on one or two of the best vacation rental companies in the waterways region will be provided with brief details on name, address, telephone and fax, price range, booking procedures and how to obtain all needed information.

A Summary of the Waterways: Selecting Your Destination

Decisions on where to travel are personal. This guidebook, supported perhaps by general country or regional guidebooks, is intended principally to present the options, to describe the waterways, and to show how to get the most enjoyment from your chosen area. We suggest that people especially interested in birds, in flora, in fishing, and in history, contact the appropriate Government Tourist Offices for information on their particular subjects of interest.

ENGLAND

There are six principal *natural* water systems in England open to extended boating and all are within easy reach of London and Heathrow and other destination cities. All are well served by a number of boatyards that provide rental cruisers (and sailing yachts at some).

Norfolk Broads

A hundred miles northwest of London, the Norfolk Broads is a 600 square mile area of lakes and intertwining rivers, including the Bure, Ant, Yare, Chet, and Waveney. Together they form Britain's newest national park. Old market towns such as Wroxham, Beccles, Horning, Acle, and St. Olaves lie along the waterways, and the navigable River Wensum penetrates to the mooring in the center of Norwich. There are walking trails through forests and fens, waterside inns and pubs and ancient sites including St. Benet's Abbey, Burgh Castle, and Berney Arms Mill. This is Britain's most popular region for boating, where boats and wherries have been rented since the late nineteenth century. It is a rich natural wildlife ecosystem and waterfowl sanctuary. Take aboard rental bicycles to explore paths and waterside towns and historic sites. All free-cruising (no locks or other restrictions). One week minimum to explore part—two weeks easily filled. Combined boat and cottage rental option available. Over thirty marinas, fifty rental motor cruiser companies and four sailing yacht boatyards in the Broads, as well as many moorings.

The Thames
The clearwater Thames River is navigable for rental motor cruisers from near Regents Park in London for 125 mile west into Gloucestershire. The closest rental marinas for foreign arrivals at Heathrow are at Thames Ditton, Datchet, and Laleham, all a short and easy taxi ride away. The main waterside towns and sites along the route include western London, Datchet, Windsor, Maidenhead, Marlow, Henley, Reading, Wallingford, Abingdon, Oxford, and Lechlade. Many important historic sites include Hampton Court, Runnymeade, Sinodun Hill, and Buscot House. Also abbeys and National Trust properties, as well as Windsor Castle and the town of Windsor. Most of the towns can be explored by foot or bicycle from the mooring and marinas along the way. There are many waterside pubs, inns and shops. This is a cultural/historical area as well as a wildlife ecosystem. Free-cruising; few locks. One week for one-way; two weeks easily spent on the round trip. Eleven rental boatyards and marinas serve the river, along with many other moorings in locations ranging from waterside inns to public parks in the town along the way.

The Severn & Avon

The River Severn flows through the heart of England, southward from Stourport near Birmingham through the city of Worcester, to its confluence with the Avon near Tewkesbury. The Avon flows southwesterly through the north Cotswolds, passing through Stratford-upon-Avon en route to its meeting with the Severn at Tewkesbury. This is tranquil, rolling countryside, with many small riverside towns and inns. One week is a typical cruising time from the one remaining boatyard at Upton-on-Severn.

Cambridgeshire

The Great Ouse River, the Cam, and Old West River flow through the towns of Bedford, Huntingdon, Ely; south into Cambridge or north into Denver. This is pastoral countryside, with historic towns and sites. Branches of the main rivers run through numerous off-track towns such as Botany Bay, Hilgay, and Wicken. Exploration is slow-paced; a week is ideal. Four rental boatyards, plus other moorings along the routes. There are two boatyards, one at St. Ives and one at Ely. One week is a typical cruise time, but there is access from the Cam to the long and complex system of canals called the Warwickshire and Leistershire Rings (principally a domain of canal boats).

The Yorshire Ouse

The Yorkshire Ouse is not a major cruising area, but is a pleasant one, especially in that it passes along the perimeter of the Yorkshire Dales National Park and through the cities of York and Ripon. The public moorings in the center of York, and at the end of navigation near the center of Ripon give boaters easy access to the two great cathedrals as well as other sights of the cities. The boat base is in York.

Lake Windermere

Windermere is a small lake, eleven miles long and one mile wide,

set in the beautiful countryside that forms England's popular Lake Country of Cumbria. Because it combines scenery, history and lakeside towns full of shops, pubs, B&Bs, self-catering cottages, water sports and hills to tempt hikers, it is one of England's most visited areas. Having stayed there on land, we especially liked staying there on the water. The single boatyard, Windermere Holidays Afloat, located at Bowness-on-Windermere, has been in the business for over fifty years. Motor cruiser and sailing yachts are available and it is a good place to learn to sail.

SCOTLAND

Often called the Caledonian Canal, which gives the wrong impression of the nature of these waters, the Highland Lakes are a sixty-mile-long chain of connected lakes (Loch Ness, Loch Oich, Loch Lochy) that fill the mountain-rimmed Great Rift from Inverness southwestward to Ft. William. The main waterside towns and sites are Inverness, Drumnadrochit Village, and Ft. Augustus, along with moorings at Urquhart Castle and Aldourie Castle. There are over a dozen lakeside inns, pubs, shops. Most of the cruising is in open water, but there are locks in short canals between the lakes. Wild beauty and calm waters characterize the region. One week at leisure should be planned for the 120-mile (195 km) round-trip journey. There are boatyards at Inverness and at Laggan Locks. Salt-water cruisers are also available for rent to take down the stairway of locks near Fort William. Unlike in fresh water, EXPERIENCE is required. Ocean cruising is not covered in this guide—contact Blakes at 1603-782911.

How to Use this Guide

Unless you know precisely where you want to go—which country, which region, which waterway—an hour or so perusing the guidebook will be a good beginning. If you have a specific destination in mind, say England's Thames, simply go directly to the appropriate chapter. In general, however, choices must be made: river or lake, wildlife sanctuaries, fishing areas, regions where the social life of waterside pubs, inns and towns call, or where castle walls stand solemnly on the shores, and monastic ruins rising from islands tell of other times? All of these, or some? Is it warm enough in April to cruise the Scottish Lochs? How about the Broads?

To help newcomers make informed decisions on where to embark on an adventure by water, each of the next five chapters are devoted to a particular geographic area open to exploration by motor cruiser or sailing yacht. Because the waterways differ from one another in terms of area or length or magnitude or shape, it follows that there may not be firm consistency in the order of subjects as they unfold in each chapter. Canals are included only when they are integral to the waterway system, perhaps between two rivers or when, like the Caledonian Canal, they connect a series of lakes such as in the Scottish Highlands.

Each regional chapter begins with an *Overview*, describing in general terms the topography of the area, the nature of the waterways, their scope and expanse, and recommendations on how long should be allotted for a reasonable itinerary. Although this is not a naturalist's handbook, there will be in each chapter a short overview of the flora and wildlife that can be expected. This will include information on the flyways and specific areas within the region where, for example, birdwatchers will likely be rewarded, or unusual plants may be found. In addition to the natural character of the waterways, their history will be touched upon, especially in terms of highlighting special historic places to visit along the route. These may range from mysterious Celtic ruins to ancient abbeys, old market towns or castles, waterpumps to eel weirs. This information can often be enhanced by use of general guidebooks to the country or region, books that deal more specifically with such topics as natural history and environmental studies.

The Search for a European Getaway

Saltwater boating is not included in the guide, although the waters off the west and southwest coasts of Scotland are well noted for their character, and boats can be taken between the Highland lakes and the sea through a remarkable steep cascade of many locks. The waters require experience in boating, and this guide is aimed more for persons who have never operated a boat before, or who have limited experience. Basically, renters for the salt water vessels are required to demonstrate some skill at chart reading and a fundamental knowledge of boating. But both sailing yachts and motor cruisers are available from the same companies included here and more specific information is readily available by contacting them.

The chapters tell about the water journey in general, written in a manner to provide a sense of what it will be like. These are the subjective views of the authors as American visitors, exploring not only the countryside, but the actuality of boating abroad. Once a region, river or lake system is decided upon, the detailed waterway navigational chart and guide should be purchased from the suitable British source shown in applicable chapter, as noted. These charts indicate every spot to tie up, every town along the route, locks if any, and most ancient sites to visit.

Where the *Overview* tells about topography, history, nature of the waters and the countryside, the *Highlights* will point out specific places of interest. For example, the *Overview* of the Southern Broads will tell of the Norwich Rivers Yare and Wensum, while the *Highlights* will tell of the mooring just below Norwich Cathedral in the center of the city. The *Highlights* note outstanding bird areas, inviting woods, a castle or abbey to explore, an historic and photogenic windpump, outstanding pub or inn for lunch or dinner, or an especially pleasant overnight mooring. References may also be made to locally available booklets and guides.

Self-discovery and exploration of the waterways is part of the fun; poring over a navigation chart or talking with boatyard staff about the best approach to the journey. And finding out where to go becomes easier as each day passes, even on the larger and more complex waterways, but especially if it is relatively small. Nevertheless, there are situations and places where an example of how time might be allotted, distances covered, stops at important sites figured in, and even nighttime moorings to aim for, is helpful, especially at the beginning. Where the waterway system, or the region, is such that an illustration or two will help in planning, then a sample *Itinerary* or two is provided. But these offer ideas, and are not meant to be adhered to at the expense of exploring some unmentioned backwater, village or ruin.

Each chapter will contain recommendations on the *Best Times to Go* visit the region. The recommended best times are based on our personal judgment, taking into account seasonal weather, crowds or lack of crowds and seasonal rental prices. Each chapter also suggests the number of days, weeks or months in advance that a boat should be booked in order to assure availability. These time frames take into account the popularity of the boating region, specific location, number of boatyards and boats available, season of the year and the size of vessel required.

The Boat Rental Company section of each chapter simply describes a selection of recommended companies that are most easily reached by foreign travelers without rental cars. Other criteria include the quality of the boatyards, the cruisers themselves, and the service. Other considerations are the ease with which groceries and supplies can be purchased nearby, and the location of the marina relative to the most desirable cruising areas.

Information on *Getting to the Boatyards* is generally provided with each section on the Boat Rental Companies and will explain the best approach to finding the boatyards, especially for travelers who do not have a car. Often, it is simply a matter to telling the company where and when you are arriving in the country—transportation can often be arranged.

The Search for a European Getaway

The information assumes arrival at Heathrow or Gatwick International Airports in England, then departure by train from London. If a car is rented, simply follow a road map to the location as it is described in the booking documents that are always sent by the boat rental company or agent.

Boatyards easily accessible from destination railway stations are especially singled out and named, although a few are most easily reached by bus or taxi. Ditton, Datchet, and Laleham, for example, are Thames riverports closer to Heathrow than is central London. This information will not only help in planning, but will make the selection of boat rental companies more manageable.

Other than accessibility and location as noted above, if there are any reasons why one or another rental operating company should be selected, they will be discussed here. For example, if a one-way itinerary is planned, then a company that has at least two boatyard bases at the desired starting and ending points must be chosen. Or perhaps we were especially impressed with a particular fleet of cruisers, or wish to point out that some classic styles are available for those who fancy tradition.

If there are any reasons why one style of cruiser might be preferable to another, these will be discussed in this section. For example, if there are some boat designs better suited to children from a perspective of safety or convenience, this will be noted. Or, when there are some designs that are more comfortable in seasons of marginal weather, or especially suited to hot weather cruising, these will be described, as will any boats especially suited to disabled persons.

The *Booking Procedure* section will provide the details necessary to obtain catalogs, maps, charts and other materials to help with planning and decision making. This is followed by information on how to handle the actual booking.

Contact Information

British Tourist Authority (BTA)
551 Fifth Avenue, Suite 701
New York, NY 10176-0799
Tel: 800-462-2748; 212-986-2200
Fax: 212-986-1188
Websites: www.visitbritain.com
www.usagateway.visitbritain.com

British Tourist Authority (BTA)
5915 Airport Rd., Suite 120
Mississauga, Ontario L4V 1T1 Canada
Tel: 888-847-4885
Fax: 905-405-1835
Website: www.visitbritain.com\ca

Northern Ireland Tourist Board
551 Fifth Avenue, 7th Floor
New York, NY 01076-0799
Tel: 800-326-0036; 212-922-0101
Fax: 212-922-0099

Northern Ireland Tourist Board
St. Anne's Court, 59 North Street
Belfast BT1 1NB
Tel: 2890-246609
Fax: 2890-240960
Website: www.ni-tourism.com

For the latest updates to *The Natural Waterways of Great Britain*, visit the book's page on Interlink's website at:
www.interlinkbooks.com/waterwaysGB.html

Telephone Information

Long Distance International Telephone Country Code (England, Wales, Scotland, Northern Ireland): Dial the international access code required from your country, then 44. From the US and Canada, the access code is 011. For example, to contact Blakes Boats in England from the US and Canada, dial 011-44-1603-739400.

For domestic calls within the UK, no access code or country code are required; however, a "0" must be added at the beginning of the ten digit phone number. Thus, to contact Blakes from within the UK, dial 01603-739400.

City Code Changes: Some city codes in Britain, and all of Northern Ireland, have changed in June 2000. London Central (old 171 from abroad, 0171 domestic) is now 207 from abroad, 0207 domestic; London outskirts (old 181) is now 208 from abroad, 0208 domestic. Exeter from abroad is 1392; Edinburgh, Scotland: 131; Bath: 1225.

Northern Ireland: Telephone Country Code is the same as rest of UK: access code +44. Belfast (city) from abroad is 28-XX + 6 digits. Example: To contact the Northern Ireland Tourist Board in Belfast dial 011-44-2890-246609. As with the rest of the UK, for domestic calling only add a "0" at the beginning of the telephone number.

NOTE: *All telephone and fax prefixes in these chapters are new, effective April 16, 2000.* For more information, see: www.numberchange.com

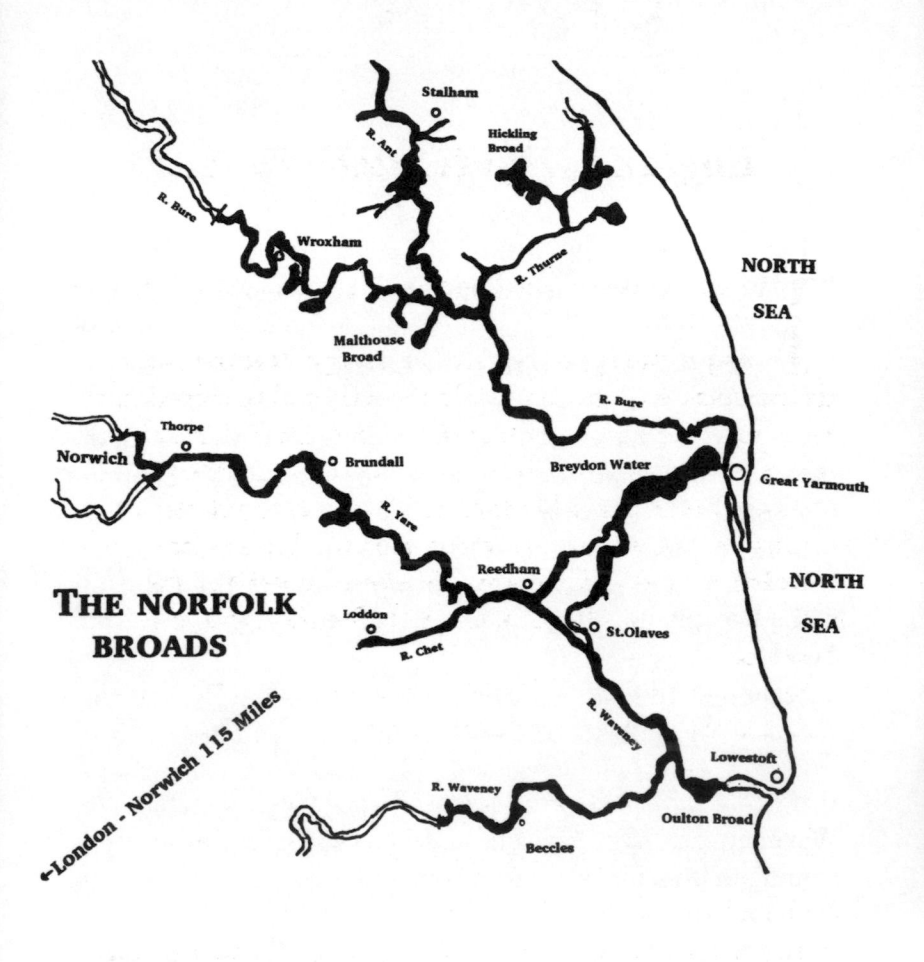

Stalham

R. Ant

Hickling
Broad

R. Bure

Wroxham

R. Thurne

NORTH

SEA

Malthouse
Broad

R. Bure

Thorpe

Norwich

Brundall

Breydon Water

Great Yarmouth

THE NORFOLK

BROADS

R. Yare

Reedham

NORTH

SEA

Loddon

St.Olaves

R. Chet

R. Waveney

Lowestoft

R. Waveney

Oulton Broad

Beccles

London - Norwich 115 Miles

CHAPTER 2

England: The Norfolk Broads

T
o the northeast of London, England bulges into the North Sea. The sea defines an area which, because of its proximity to continental Europe and the nature of its lowlands, was easy and early to settle and to subsequently be conquered by most anyone who had an interest in doing so. It's called East Anglia, and within its bounds are the counties of Essex, Suffolk, and Norfolk. It is Norfolk, the northeastern county of this region, to which pleasure boaters have long traveled, a land of waterways in whose center lies the great cathedral city of Norwich, about 100 miles (160 km) from London.

Through this region of some 400 square miles (1,035 sq km) flow six placid rivers, the Ant, the Bure, the Thurne, Yare, Waveney, and the Chet, plus a short section of the Wensum that divides the city of Norwich. Two of these, the Bure and Waveney, are large enough to be navigable by larger ships coming in from the sea, but the others are restricted to pleasure craft and the working boats of those who live there. These rivers, along with a watery assortment of lakes, ditches, dikes, channels, marshlands and meadowlands, form what is known collectively as the Broads.

"Broads" are expanses of water, specifically the fairly shallow lakes formed in vast areas of East Anglia, where for centuries peat was removed by the Saxons and Normans.

Like the rivers, individual broads have names—Malthouse Broad, Hickling Broad, Salhouse Broad—and they serve as home for a multitude of wildlife, water birds, and migratory fowl. Add Rollesby Broad, Sutton Broad, Martham Broad, Filby Broad, Horsey Mere, Hoveton Little Broad, Strumpshire Broad, and Reedham Water to the many others and it becomes clear the scope of this waterland. The purpose of this chapter is not to attempt to describe them all, nor the details of all the rivers, but to provide an enticing overview and show the means by which traveling through the area can be accomplished. Indeed, self-discovery is a key to the pleasures of cruising here, and booklets, maps and pamphlets abound in the region, produced by such organizations as the Broads Authority, English Nature, and the Norfolk Wildlife Trust. They are available at booksellers, boatyards, and at the seven Broads Authority Information Centres dotted throughout the waterways. So rich and varied is this sanctuary that in 1978 it became Britain's newest equivalent to a national park.

The landscape is dotted with windmills, or more accurately windpumps, some of which were used for draining the marshes for transformation into grazing meadows, and some for keeping water channels at the levels needed to allow the commerce of boats, ships, and barges. Materials, supplies, and goods of all sorts were moved between the manufacturing and market towns of East Anglia, and accessed the sea at the ports of Great Yarmouth and Lowestoft. With the development of rail, the importance of the waterways waned and shipping became mostly a memory. Yet well into this century the area called the Broads was home to trappers of eels who caught the creatures commercially and for their own use. The eels spawn here, then swim to sea, where they seem to disappear into the sweep and depths of the Atlantic, only to come back home to the channels of the Broads and spawn a new generation, maintaining the mysterious, ancient cycle. The strangeness of life in the Broads, even in near contemporary times, has been beautifully described in English writer Graham Swift's novel, *Waterland*, which was later made into a movie of the same name starring Jeremy Irons.

As with many vast water systems, the Broads abounds with birds, some resident, others migratory, all a source of enjoyment to boaters who come either to share the environment or to seriously observe. No one travels at a fast pace, and many boaters rent a small dory to tow, the better to look into backwaters too restrictive and delicate to navigate in the larger cruisers. Others rent bicycles to carry aboard to explore lowland paths or waterside towns.

The majority of the towns of Norfolk and north Suffolk have grown along the waterways and broads, many of them picturesque, such as Beccles, Loddon, and Ludham. The greatest gem of the area is Norwich, a city with more beautiful medieval churches within its boundaries than any other British city save London. The Norwich cathedral thrusts its spire to a height second in England only to Salisbury. The River Wensum, a short distance from its confluence with the Yare, runs through the heart of the city where there is a mooring for pleasure boats near Pull's Ferry, a picturesque point that at one time was the fortified water gate into the city. In all, the center of Norfolk is one of the most popular destinations for boaters of the Broads.

Many other engaging waterside towns with their inns, pubs, grocers and other suppliers, can be reached from moorings available to boaters. Fine historic sites are scattered about the area, many accessible from the water's edge: St. Benet's Abbey on the banks of the Bure, the remains of the third-century Roman Burgh Castle (see River Waveney) on Breydon Water, and especially fine churches at Ranworth, St. Michael's, Ludham and Oulton Broad.

In modern times the Broads seems to be home to almost as many pleasure boats as it is to herons, but in the way of this private bird, the boats do not crowd the expanse.

In the U.S.:

British Tourist Authority (BTA)
551 Fifth Avenue, Suite 701
New York, NY 10176-0799
Tel: 800-462-2748; 212-986-2200
Fax: 212-986-1188
Website: www.visitbritain.com

In Canada:

British Tourist Authority (BTA)
5915 Airport Road, Suite 120
Mississauga, Ontario L4V 1T1
Tel: 888-847-4885; 905-405-1840
Fax: 905-405-1835

In the U.K.:

The Broads Authority
18 Colegate
Norwich, Norfolk NR3 1BQ
United Kingdom

Other useful websites:
www.norfolkbroads.com/homepage.htm
www.norfolkbroads.com/guide/boaters.htm
www.yacht.co.uk/

for accommodations:
www.s-h-systems.co.uk
www.queensmoat.com

The development of the area as the most popular cruising and sailing center of Great Britain began shortly after the turn of the century when an enter-prising resident, Harry Blake, let it be known that boats could be rented for the pleasure of anyone who wished to sail on the Broads. The small variety of boats, we understand, included both rowing dinghies, punts and, for sailors, wherries, which are flat-bottomed shallow draft sailboats. The venture was an obvious success because the business is still in operation after nearly ninety years and has expanded enormously.

This is an ideal boating area for anyone who has never before operated a motor cruiser, much less a sailing yacht. The waters are quiet and combine wide lock-free rivers and lake expanses, plus a few narrows that need only be entered after some experience and confidence have been gained. It is an area that can be enjoyed with a minimum of attention to the helm and boat operation, allowing a maximum of attention to the surroundings. Yet it is also an area that can uplift the more experienced sailor who rents a more challenging sailing yacht and tacks through the winds.

Character and Fauna of the Broads: Fens, Carr, Forest and Meadowland

Think of the Broads as a series of concentric zones, starting with open water, surrounded by the reed marshes of the fens, surrounded by scrub and semi-forested carr, and finally surrounded by either meadowland (often referred to as grazing marshes) or dryland forest of deciduous trees, mostly oak. Of course the zones are not regular in shape, and there are meanders of the rivers, intersections by dikes, fingers of forest, hillocks, even constructed cuts. But the idea helps characterize the complex and unusual nature of the Broads.

The fens are wide areas of usually treeless wetland along open water, marshes where reeds and sedges dominate. These are hard areas to explore on foot, often boggy, often hardly more than a thin layer of roots and plants overlaying liquid, yet besides the birdlife they support, they are complex ecosystems in which a multitude of plants grow: meadowsweet, ragged robin, marsh marigolds, willow herb, and our favorite, the delicate fen orchids. They are best explored by boat, carefully nudging into what is likely shallow water, or if photography is the goal, by taking the dinghy in rather than the cruiser. These are delicate areas and must be dealt with gently. Reeds of the fens are the nesting place for black-headed gulls who build on the surface, for reed and sedge warblers whose nests surround the stalks, and for the resident bearded tits and reed buntings.

The fens are also home to many insects, from the ubiquitous dragonflies to the more rare Norfolk aeshna dragonfly, and numerous butterflies, including the swallowtail. Despite this, we were never bothered on board by gnats, no-see'ems, mosquitoes or other bothersome flying creatures.

Carr is what in America we might call wet woodlands, or perhaps swampy woods, where, larger growth has taken root than in the fens, ranging from scrub alder to sallow and birch. These areas, principally lying along the River Waveney in the South Broads and the Rivers Bure and Ant in the north, are the transition zone between fen and dryland forest. Like the fens, carr is hard to walk through and can be damaged in the process, but from the water its character and wildlife can be seen, experienced, and photographed. Look for woodcock, woodpeckers, redpolls, siskin, and blackcaps, especially along the narrower and more remote River Waveney, downstream of the town of Beccles.

Meadows, or as they are referred to in some writings, grazing marshes, are expansive areas whose character varies with the season. They are lands reclaimed for use by livestock and commercial growing from the lowlands that comprise much of the Broads. Great wind pumps, like the Berney Arms

Mill in the south, served to drain and lift marsh water into rivers and channels behind constructed dikes to be carried out to sea. As the water was drained and the land dried, it settled to the point where much of it is below the level of the rivers and lakes; that is, below the sight of passing boaters. The long dikes in several areas make for ideal walking paths, with a water environment on one hand and meadowland on the other. As summer advances and the winter wetness disappears, the wildlife of the grazing marshes changes from waders like lapwing, snipe and redshank to skylarks, owls and harriers, the latter depending on the return of mice and voles to the drying land.

Readings: *Old English Inns of East Anglia*, Daric Enterprises, High Wycombe 1987; *Water Transport in Norfolk*, Norfolk Heritage, Gressenhall, Dereham, Norfolk NR20 4DR; *Bill Oddie's Guide to the Norfolk Broads*, Oddie, English Tourist Board. These are available in Norfolk booksellers and boat rental companies; also, check the boat catalogs for ordering booklets, charts, and other information in advance.

Birds of the Broads Waters

Of special interest to North Americans are the migratory species that do not travel the North American flyways, yet inhabit the Broads en route north and southbound. Among these, Egyptian and Greylag geese are most prominent and can be seen in virtually all the Broads rivers and lakes, especially during nesting from late May to mid-June. Great Crested Grebes, called by nineteenth century writer Lubbock "the greatest ornament of the Norfolk Broads," arrive in late February and March, at which time they display their fantastic pre-mating dance. By mid-autumn, eggs have hatched and most adults and young have departed the Broads. Other open water fowl are Mute Swans, Teal, Coots, and Canada Geese; Kingfishers, Common Terns, and swift Black-headed Gulls occupy the air.

Three important birds to look for are the hard-to-spot Water Rail and Bittern, and especially the rarer Redshank which, like the striking Lapwing, can best be seen in the winter months. A most sought after sighting is the feeding encounter with a Marsh Harrier pair. At nesting time from late May to mid-June the female stays with the eggs or the young while the cock is on the hunt; when he returns, rather than go to the nest he circles and calls, at which point the hen rises to meet him and they pirouette in the air as the prey is handed off. We observed this exciting scene in the South Broads on the Waveney downriver of St. Olaves and again on the Yare between Berney Arms Mill and the Haddiscoe Cut in early June.

Everyone with even a mild interest in birds should purchase the small booklet *Birds of the Norfolk Broads*, Reg Jones ISBN 0-7117-0180-6, available at any bookstore in the county of Norfolk.

Planning from Abroad

Despite being the most popular inland cruising and sailing waters of Britain, planning from a distance is more complex than for any other areas of Britain, just because of the sheer size of the area, its many rivers and lakes, and the numerous boatyards to choose from. To explore the entire Broads by boat, giving the area the attention it deserves, requires at least two or, better, three weeks. As this may exceed the amount of time overseas visitors can devote to cruising or sailing, we will divide the region in two, the North and the South. From this, a boatyard can be selected depending on which area you want to explore. If you plan to rent a car, peruse in their entirety the

Hoseasons and Blakes catalogs; if traveling by rail, look only to the boatyards in the locations either profiled or listed below that are easily reached from a railway station.

Basically, with the exception of Hickling Broad and the waters of the Upper River Thurne, the northern Broads can be characterized as being busier than the southern. A more social area, it is popular with British boaters who especially enjoy the towns, pubs, inns, and markets. The southern expanse is less populated, both in terms of towns and boats; the area tends more toward the natural and the isolated, and is rich with the birdlife that shuns human habitation.

The second key decision for anyone arriving in Britain from abroad, especially anyone boating for the first time, is to choose the most desirable and accessible starting points from among the five dozen or so possibilities. As there is little use in having a rental car standing idle during cruising time, this generally means a boatyard near a railway station in Norfolk served from London. Although this results in fewer boatyards and boats to choose from, both are sufficient in number that availability may only be a problem during the peak season. The selection of which boatyard location is of course less important if you are renting a car.

There are roughly sixty-five boat rental enterprises operating from some thirty-two boatyard marinas in the Broads; just six offer sailing yachts as well as motor cruisers. The sailing yachts are available through Blakes and are located at Upton, Martham, Horning, St. Olaves and two at Wroxham.

For convenience, the boatyards of the North Broads and the South Broads are noted separately in this chapter under the appropriate geographic headings. They do not include all the boatyards, but the ones selected are highlighted because, among other factors, they are accessible by rail.

There may be a modest fee if booking through a US company, but service is generally faster and more personalized.

British Agents:

- Blakes Holidays Ltd.
  Tel: 1603-739400; Fax: 1603-782871
  E-mail: boats@blakes.co.uk
  Website: www.blakes.co.uk

- Hoseasons Holidays Ltd.
  Lowestoft, Suffolk NR32 3LT, England
  Tel: 1502-501010; Fax: 1502-586781
  E-mail: mail@hoseasons.co.uk
  Website: www.hoseasons.co.uk

North American Agents for Blakes:

- Great Trips Unlimited
  Tel: 888-329-9720; Fax: 503-297-5308
  E-mail: admin@gtunlimited.com
  Website: www.gtunlimited.com

- Blakes Vacations
  Tel: 800-628-8118; Fax: 847-244-8118
  E-mail: blakes1076@aol.com
  Website: www. blakesvacations.com

North American Agents for Hoseasons & Connoisseur:

- Jody Lexow Yacht Charters
  Tel: 800-662-2628; Fax: 401-845-8909
  E-mail: jlyc@edgenet.com
  Website: www.jodylexowyachtcharters.com

North American Agents for Connoisseur:

- Le Boat
  Tel: 800-922-0291
  E-mail: leboatinc@worldnet.att.net
  Website: www.leboat.com

Getting to the Boatyards

Besides the pleasure of traveling by cruiser or sailboat there is the economic advantage of not having to rent a car. The only problem is that not all of the Broads boatyards are convenient to a railway station. While British residents have the advantage of driving to any of the boatyards, foreign visitors traveling by rail are somewhat limited.

We generally do not recommend one cruiser company over another unless there are compelling distinctions between quality of boats, style of boats, maintenance, equipment, and supplies on board, breadth of selection, quality of service, and the like. One criterion, however, applies to travelers who come from a considerable distance overseas and who do not have a rental vehicle or a means of transportation arranged by the boat companies. The criterion is **convenience**. The ease of getting to the final destination town or boatyard site from airline gateway cities such as London and Manchester, or rail hubs readily accessible to overseas visitors. It also means access in the boatyard area to accommodations in which to spend a night or so prior to the cruise start day and ease in buying provisions for the cruise.

There are, nevertheless, a number of boat rental companies whose boatyards are easily accessible by rail, a large enough selection that this does not appreciably diminish your choice of boat sizes or styles.

The principal boatyard towns in the North Broads that are served by rail are *Wroxham* and *Acle*; in the South Broads they are *Lowestoft, Beccles, Reedham, St. Olaves,* and *Brundall*. For sailing yachts, the only two boatyards convenient to a rail terminal are Brinkcraft Yachts at Wroxham and The Traditional Broads Yacht Company in the South Broads at St. Olaves, both available for booking through Blakes. These seven towns are all connected to London's Liverpool Station, but all require a change of trains: at Norwich for the northern towns and at Ipswich for those in the South Broads. There are numerous departures daily and each route is equally convenient.

For towns not served by rail, some boat companies provide transportation from the station to the boatyard, such as New Horizon Holidays, for example, does for its Stalham marina. If you find a cruiser or company you want that is not in a rail town, inquire about transportation.

In sum, for travelers by rail the number of Broads boatyards from which to choose a motor cruiser has been reduced from about sixty-five to thirty-six, of which fifteen are in the north and twenty-one in the south. For sailing yachts, the boatyards have been reduced from six to two. Selecting which company and which boat has become easier, but still requires some pleasant mulling. Final details such as finding your way to the boatyard from the nearest railway station is best handled by contacting the renting company by phone, fax, or e-mail for instructions.

Once a cruising area is chosen, and an accessible boatyard is selected and contacted, the rail itinerary can be worked out, either by referring to the Cooks Timetable or by the much easier method of contacting Rail Express:

Rail Pass Express
Point-to-point ticket information: Tel: 614-793-7650
(9:00 AM–3:00 PM EST M-F); www.railpass.com; e-mail: relations@railpass.com
For rail passes & point-to-point tickets: Tel: 800-722-7151

For example, if you are planning to arrive at Heathrow and have chosen a cruise company in Horning (near Wroxham /Hoveton), tell the Rail Express agent that you want tickets from London to Wroxham/Hoveton in Norfolk. They will do the rest. If doing it yourself, the rail route is London (Liverpool Station)-Ipswich-Norwich-Wroxham. If you want information directly, telephone Anglia Railways at 345-484950 or, for booking and payment by credit card, 1603-764776. If you do this directly, work well in advance. We advise purchasing in North America before departure for Britain by contacting Rail Pass Express.

If planning to travel on by rail from the Wroxham area,

the Bittern Line operates a nice train north to the coastal towns of Cromer and Sheringham.

If you find a cruiser line in the Blakes, New Horizon or Hoseasons catalogs that strikes your fancy but is not near one of the rail-serviced towns included here, there is bus service between Norwich and a string of towns to the northeast including Wroxham, Horning, Ludham, Hickling, Stalham and Sutton. If the bus is of interest, ask the reservations office at Blakes, Hoseasons or the boat company for information, or telephone the Norwich Bus Information Centre at 1692-500-626116 or Neaves Coaches at 1692-580383.

If renting a car is more appealing, but there are budget considerations, one approach is to rent one-way. Rental prices are relatively high in the UK, but drop-off charges are minimal. If there are no budget constraints, then there are no limitations on the start point. Vehicles can be safely stored at the boatyards.

Choice of Cruiser Styles

There are literally dozens of motor cruiser layouts, dimensions and styles, all made clear in the catalogs. Look for the characteristics that appeal, but that also answer specific questions: Do you want maximum cabin space at the expense of deck space? Or vice-versa? If there are children in your family or group, which vessels have the highest, safest rails or cockpit depths? Single or double berths? Is the berth layout suitable for privacy, as in separate cabins, or will your need be filled by having some berths convertible from dining seats or a sofa-bed? The answers to these will tell you something about day use space, places for children's naps, whether or not you must re-make the beds every night. Carefully study the layout schemes in the brochures and catalogs.

Also consider the time of year—if you are traveling in the winter, or early in the season when weather is marginal, then enclosed space is more desirable. In summer, larger outside decks are more desirable.

There are many variations, but basically two styles of boat are available on the Broads. The typical *Broads cruiser* has a forward or middle helm position, the cabin space occupies almost all of the hull, and there is a sliding top over the salon area. On dry days the roof can be opened, exposing the living-dining area, and often the helm seat, to the sky. These are the best boats if there are small children, and they maximize inside space, almost like a low contoured houseboat, but not so clumsy. A drawback is that unless there is a large clear window or door at the rear and an open passage behind the helm, it can be hard to see behind. Most of the newer designs have overcome the problem, but ask before booking if there is clear rear view from the helm. The dual helm version of the Broads cruiser has an inside forward helm position and an upper after position, open to the air. These are usually larger, more luxurious boats. Ideally, they should have exit/entry doors both fore and aft. Check for this, because if there is no forward door it could mean walking along a narrow strip to get to and from the bow and the bow lines.

Besides their maneuverable character, the sliding-roof cruisers are of special interest if planning your cruise in the winter or the early months of spring or late fall; they afford protection in case of inclement weather, yet slide widely open on sunny days.

The other style is a *sport cruiser* design, the kind most often seen in pleasure craft marinas around the world, with an aft (rear) cockpit and helm. In some the steering position is inside the cabin, good for protection from the weather, yet with all-around visibility. In the other version, the cockpit is open and can be covered with a folding canopy. Of the two sport designs, we prefer the former, especially given the idiosyncrasies of weather on the Broads.

Given that the Broads rivers are slow, with no locks, and low speed limits, maneuverability is of little concern, so don't worry about the boat being too large and therefore less agile. The only time to consider size is if you want to get under the low Potter Heigham Bridge into the upper Thurne and the nature reserves at Hickling Broad and Horsey Mere. The bridge is a medieval structure that cannot accommodate many of the larger cruisers (see the River Thurne in the North Broads section).

Although there were only two of us, we preferred a bit more space than is usually available on the very smallest boats. On the South Broads, the sliding top cruisers designed for four, such as Castle Craft's Kenilworth and Stirling Castle, gave the two of us the luxury of substantial space and could easily have accommodated two more persons. They are model modern Broads cruisers.

Best Times to Go

The winter months can be cold and dreary in East Anglia, so unless you are willing to accept gray weather in exchange for isolation and low boat prices, we suggest not going before early April (but avoid Easter week). May to the middle of June and again from early September to mid-October are optimum in terms of weather, fewer numbers of boats on the Broads and fewer numbers of tourists in the streets, as well as lower prices for everything from motor cruisers and sailing yachts to restaurant meals. The summer peak period begins the last week of July and lasts until the end of August.

The school year in Britain ends later than in the US, so summer season crowds and rates also begin later there, making the first two weeks of June generally ideal for a visit. Study the catalogs carefully, though: not only for the best rate periods but for odd peak price times that often occur on British "Bank Holidays," and other holidays for which there is no counterpart in the US. In all, there are nine different price bands tied to the seasons and holidays.

Advance Booking Times

Peak season (July 15–August 30)	3 mos
Early summer (June 15–July 15)	3 mos
Early Autumn (August 30–Sept. 15)	2 mos
Shoulder seasons (May)	2 wks
Low season (March, early May, Sept 15–30)	1 wk
Off season (Jan through April, Oct.–mid-Dec.)	1 wk

The North Broads

Highlights
The River Bure

Wroxham & Hoveton are the principal center of boating and provisioning in the North Broads, and the Bure is the principal river, busiest in terms of boatyards and boats. The two towns, actually more like a single town divided by the river, have between them over a dozen rental boat companies in marinas stretching along the beautiful upper Bure from above the Wroxham Bridge downriver five miles to the pretty little town of **Horning**. Besides the railway station in Wroxham, there is bus service to the Horning-based boatyards of King Line, Woods Dyke, Norfolk Broads Yachting Co. and Ferry Boatyard, and upriver through Belaugh (Belaugh Boats) to the end of navigation at **Coltishall**.

The town center itself is not a place with ancient dwellings, churches and other buildings but, rather, it seems that the entire community is geared toward boating, with everything from a riverside supermarket to restaurants, outfitters, pubs, hotels, and B&Bs. It is also the site of the main offices of the boating agent giant, Blakes. It is an excellent starting point for exploring the northern area, including the Rivers Bure, Ant, and Thurne, as well as numerous broads, villages, and wildlife areas.

Because of the railroad station at Wroxham/Hoveton, this is also the most convenient North Broads starting point for anyone arriving from overseas and depending on rail to get to the boatyards.

Although Wroxham/Hoveton is not a town where several days can be spent sightseeing, it's still nice to arrive a day early and spend a night in a hotel in the vicinity of your departure point. In town, stop at the **Information Centre** on Station Road (a block off the main street), not only for material on Wroxham and Hoveton, the **Craft Centre** and two very old churches, but on the Broads overall. The center is operated by the Broads Authority. A company called Roy's of Wroxham (although it's in Hoveton) dominates the town center and makes provisioning for your cruise very easy. Hotels convenient to the railway station and many boatyards in Wroxham/Hoveton include:

- Hotel Wroxham
  Tel: 1603-782061; Fax: 1603-784279
  www.ecn.co.uk/hotelwroxham
  moderately priced; ask for river front room

- King's Head Hotel
  Tel: 1603-782429; Fax: 1603-784622
  economy

- Broads Hotel
  Tel: 1603-782869
  modest

- Swan Hotel, Lower Street, Horning
  Tel: 1692-630316
  traditional hotel; near boatyards

- Norfolk Mead Hotel, Coltishal (near Belaugh)

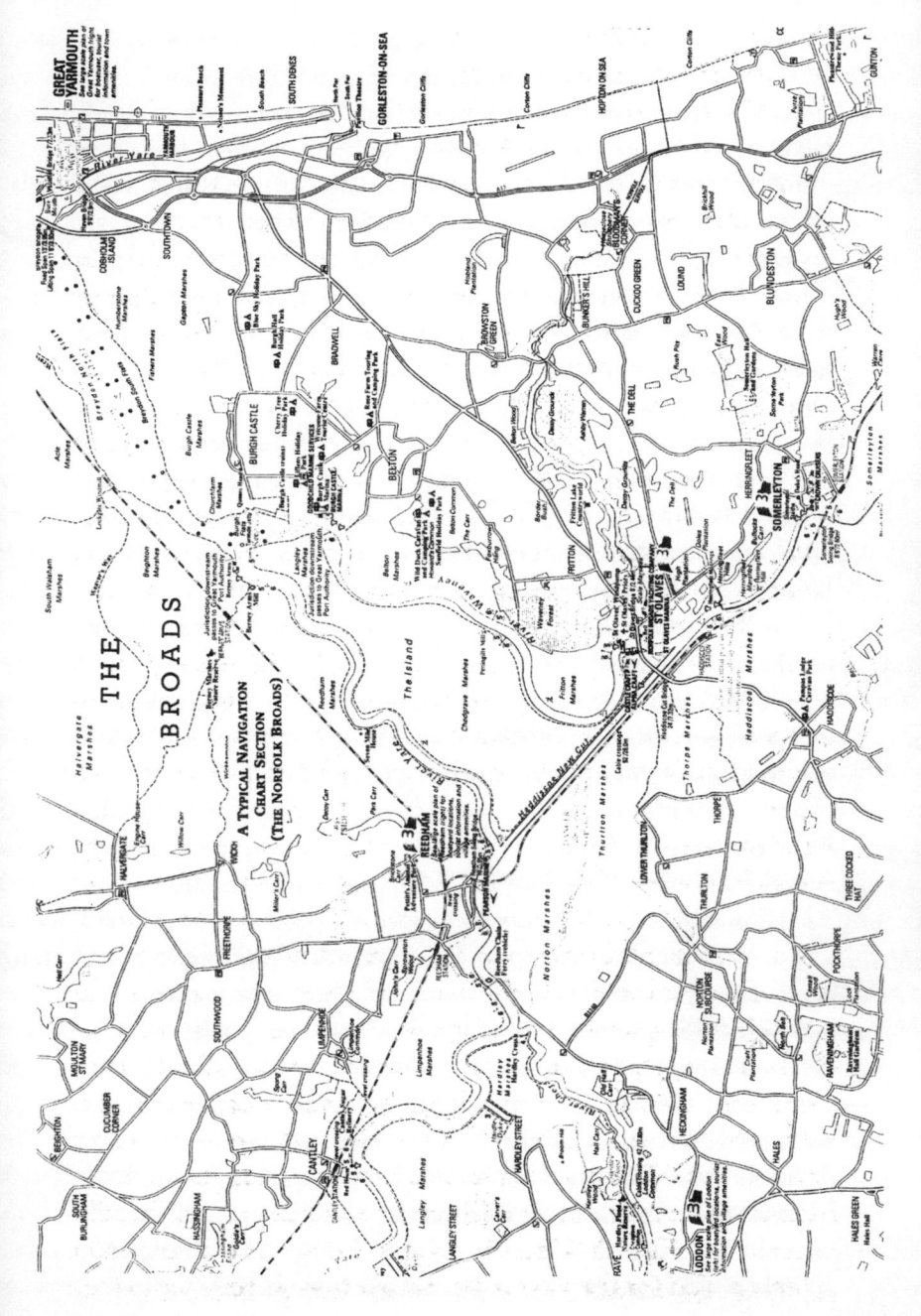

Tel: 1603-737531

very attractive manor-type hotel

The Wroxham-Hoveton bridge is a good starting point for measuring distances on the Broads. The Bure is navigable upriver from the bridge for seven miles to where the Coltishall Lock marks the end of hire-cruiser navigation. This stretch is an exquisite series of meanders through forested countryside, past waterside homes, small parks, and the hamlet of **Belaugh** and to the village of **Coltishall** where there are antique shops, riverside pubs, and a very nice mooring at the Coltishall Common. A good spot for the first night out after a late start. Downriver from the bridge the Bure flows twenty-four miles, almost to the sea at the city of Great Yarmouth. For boaters not wanting to go upstream on the first day out, an ideal first night mooring, depending on the time of your start, is the small and tranquil mooring at **St. Benedict's** (1½ hours from Wroxham, 20 minutes from Horning).

At the end of a cut from the river's south shore some fifteen minutes beyond St. Benedict's, the small **Malthouse Broad** opens up, surrounded on three sides by the **Bure Marshes Nature Reserve.** At the south end, the hamlet of Ranworth offers a substantial public marina with all facilities needed by boaters. Next to a combined Blakes Boating and public information office stands a small restaurant and tiny grocery, across from which is a very good pub, the Malthouse itself.

This is an important stop: walk the pathways and boardwalks to the **Broadland Conservation Centre,** a floating house on the edge of the **Ranworth Broad** where volunteers answer questions and show all manner of displays about the environment. The center also operates a small, electrically-powered skiff that offers silent trips through the wonderful wetlands. Boardwalks also allow for the quiet exploration of the fens and carr at the edges of the broad. Photographers should have a camera ready. Walk back to the marina by way of one of the gems of the Broads, ancient **St. Helen's Church,** famous for its rood screen and paintings, and for the view of the Broads from its tower, which is a prominent guide to finding your way there. Have a scone and coffee in their tiny visitor center & tea room.

The River Ant flows into the Bure from the north, the confluence under half an hour downriver from the Malthouse cut. A cruise along its roughly nine mile navigable length is rewarding, along a gentle stream lined at its southern end with reed marshes (and marshland birdlife). From midway, low hills rise into carr and forest. Stops going or coming should include the tiny eel fisher's cottage museum at **Toad Hole,** and for walks in the nature preserve at **How Hill.** These are well marked on the navigation charts. Pace your travel, and on the way upriver check out the possible night moorings at **Irstead** and at **Neatishead** so that they can be returned to for a peaceful stay. Much better than having to spend the night at the moorings at the busy highway towns of Sutton or Stalham, or the Wayford Bridge at the far north end of navigation. These two towns, however, are good stops for a short visit, especially if you need supplies. The hamlets of Irstead and Neatishead are themselves lovely villages, the latter being the largest, with two shops, a restaurant, pub, and churches. If beginning your cruise from a boatyard at Sutton, Stalham, or Wayford Bridge, be sure to stop at Toad Hole and How Hill when outbound.

Down the Bure from the Ant mouth, a cruise into the **Walsham Broad** and a walk to the Fairhaven Garden is worthwhile before continuing down the Bure past the impressive ninth-century riverside ruin of St. Benet's Abbey, then to the juncture with the Thurne.

The River Thurne is a relatively large river into which the Bure forms a T, the joined pair retaining the name Bure all the way to its end at Great Yarmouth some three hours to the south. Up the Thurne lies only some eight miles of cruising river, but a full day of exploration if all the branches and broads are taken in.

The first mooring upriver is only five minutes away at

Thurne, a small village where some boaters rent bicycles at the Thurne *staithe* (a word of Saxon origin, meaning mooring, commonly used in the Broads).

A turn into the village of **Ludham** is the first main branch off the main river stem, an attractive old Broads town where there is a good *staithe* at Womack Water and a boatyard, Ludham Marine. Supplies are available, the thirteenth-century St. Catherine's church is certainly worth a visit, and walks follow the Ludham Marshes Nature Reserve, and go up and around How Hill. At this point, the Rivers Ant and Thurne are parallel, half a mile apart. Most important is the Hickling Broad, at two square miles (including the verges) the largest of the broads.

As we mentioned earlier, boaters on the Thurne must beware of the **Potter Heigham Old Bridge**, about an hour upstream, a medieval structure that cannot accommodate many of the larger cruisers. It is so low and so tricky that commercial sailing wherries often had to be loaded with stones to sink them low enough to make it through. These days there is a pilot to help boaters through, but some of the sport and larger Broads cruisers are simply too high. Travelers wanting to go beyond the bridge into the extensive waterway system *must rent a boat designed to make it under the bridge*. The greatest reward for the effort will accrue to lovers of nature, persons for whom the silent, unsullied waters of the vast **Hickling Broad**, the **Nature Reserve** there, and the birdlife of **Horsey Mere**, and the great **Horsey Windpump** are among the important things of life. The Hickling Broad has been a nature preserve for more than half a century, so it is a mature sanctuary for a great variety of plants, animals, insects, and birdlife. Look especially for the avocet, the marsh harrier and, in June and July, the swallowtail butterfly that depends for life on the milk parsley that thrives there. These waters beyond the bridge are the most unpopulated by other boaters, although there are often many yachts at sail. The **Horsey**

Mere Nature Reserve seems especially appealing to migrant birds who are attracted to its semi-saline waters and proximity to the sea. We understand that the old bridge serves as a water gate, controlling flow throughout the northeastern broads and the Thurne, and that its removal and replacement risks an environmental imbalance. (We can't attest to this, but it suggests the splendid attitude of the Broads Authority and environmentalists toward the Broads.) There is a mooring at **Martham,** and the outstanding **St. Mary's Church.**

The Bure continues gently past its confluence with the Thurne toward the sea, past the old **Upton Mill** and **Olby Mill** and the small, scattered village of **Upton,** where at the end of a very narrow channel there is a nice mooring and the boatyard of Eastwood Whelpton. Nature walkers can make it along paths into the **Upton Fen Nature Preserve.** This stretch of the river, roughly three hours of non-stop cruising to its end in an estuary formed behind the city of Great Yarmouth, is not its most exciting as the countryside is mostly flat downriver of the **Acle Bridge.** From the good mooring and inn at the bridge there is a mile long footpath across the marshes and dikes into the market town of Acle. There is rail service to Acle from Norwich, a trip of twenty minutes, with several departures daily. Once in town, it's a short taxi run to the Hoseasons and Blakes cruiser boatyards: **Acle Ferry Boats, Horizon Craft, Anchorcraft,** and **Bridgecraft** at the bridge. The main market day is Thursday, but it's a nice village at any time. There is no mooring in central Acle. If arriving a day early, try the **Forte Travelodge**, Acle ByPass, Acle, Tel: 1493-751970.

Downriver of Acle, the Bure flows easterly and forms what is normally considered the southern border of the North Broads. That is, its end at Great Yarmouth is about as far as boaters planning a one-week itinerary out of one of the North Broads boatyards usually plan to go before returning upriver to the home base. Beyond Acle, there are only two moorings, one at

Stokesby, an unspoiled small village where there is a pub, a few shops, **St. Andrew's Church** and a candle making center. The church is old and unusual, with a circa-1200 tower and thatched roof. The next mooring is at the picturesque, restored **Stracey Arms Windpump,** where there is a historic display. Then it's about nine miles through featureless reed marshes where the river is shallow and navigation is guided by a series of posts.

The river's end is at the confluence with the River Yare at Vauxhall Bridge in the center of the city of **Great Yarmouth.** It is a seaport and seaside holiday city, an urban shock after the peace of the waterways and Broads villages. The goal of **Great Yarmouth** may not be worth the three hours or so spent cruising from the **Stracey Arms Windpump** and return, if you take our meaning. We do not, however, discourage traveling along any segment of the waterways because a decision to continue on or turn back depends on time available, weather and other unpredictable criteria. And there is always the unexpected: the thrill of spotting the whirlwind air dance as marsh harriers pass food from one to the other. This might well be seen in June on this flat stretch of the Bure, or the verges of the vast Breydon Water just to the south.

Itineraries

Consider the North Broads as a tree, with the River Bure as its trunk and with the Ant and the Thurne as its two main branches, both on one side. Numerous cuts and smaller lakes form its minor branches and nubs. A typical one-week journey will follow the Bure from the upriver end of navigation at Coltishall to near its mouth at Great Yarmouth. From the trunk, cruise up and back along the branches, and from along branches go in and out of the many smaller stems that end in villages, mills, preserves, and dikes. Start at any of the boatyards that lie along the trunk or the branches, but the one chosen must be the one returned to, as there are no North Broads cruiser companies having two boatyards in the north to enable one-way cruises.

As noted in the section on *Getting to the Boatyards*, for travelers without a car the rail service to Wroxham/Hoveton makes the boatyards there by far the most convenient. In addition to the marinas in that twin community, there are several just a ten-minute taxi trip downriver at Horning, and one five minutes upriver at Belaugh. It is these boat companies, based on convenience, that we must recommend to readers planning a week-long North Broads journey.

The following itinerary serves only as an illustration of how a journey can be planned. Many unknowns and variables affect the plan: long summer days or shorter ones of spring and autumn; weather; early to bed and early to rise, or vice-versa. Personal interests mean that some of us like to cruise idly, stopping at everything, while others like a faster, steadier pace, and still others may spend hours walking nature paths or village shops. There is no set way, and in discovery is the fun.

Day 1. Given this starting point, after a first day occupied with checking in, receiving operating instructions, practicing on the river with an instructor, studying charts, boarding luggage and buying and stowing provisions, the best first night mooring is usually one that is nearby. For cruisers out of Belaugh or Wroxham, this means a 1½-hour upriver cruise for the very nice mooring at the Coltishall Common, where a pub dinner might be appealing. Downriver, an ideal first night mooring, depending on the time of your start, is the small and tranquil mooring at St. Benedict's, also about 1½ hours from Wroxham. There are no facilities there, but the wildfowl spend the night in a water by-way. At the end of a cut from the river's south shore some fifteen minutes beyond St. Benedict's, at the end of Malthouse Broad is Ranworth, a substantial public marina with all facilities and services needed by boaters.

Day 2. Explore the River Ant and its branches from the mouth to the northern end, stopping at the high points along the way. If the moorings at the north towns are of no interest, return in the evening as far as the Neatishead or Irstead moorings.

Day 3. Return to the Bure, cruise downriver to the Thurne and turn northward. If your cruiser has been selected with the dimensions to allow it to get under the bridge at Potter Heigham, travel into the Horsey Mere and great Hickling Broad Nature Reserves. There is a mooring at the former and three moorings in the latter. If the cruiser is too high for the bridge, return downriver and moor at Ludham for the night.

Day 4. If coming from Hickling Broad, where most of the day has been spent on the nature trails, at the Reserve Visitors Centre and aboard the reed-lighter (a special two-hour water trails cruise), overnight at Ludham. Boaters who don't go into Hickling Broad can return to the Bure and usually head downstream for Acle, Stokesby, and Stracey Arms Windpump. From there, it's a choice of going on to moorings in Great Yarmouth, or speeding up to make it to a mooring at either Reedham or St. Olaves in the South Broads. It is about four hours steady cruising from Stracey Arms to either, and it's necessary to allow time to go around the bend at Great Yarmouth into the River Yare and Breydon Water and across this expansive semi-salty estuary of the Yare. There are no moorings along the tidal Breydon Water. At its seaward end is the Breydon Water Nature Reserve, whose long shores are marshlands. An alternative to proceeding on to Breydon Water and Reedham or St. Olaves is to return to an upriver mooring, possibly Acle.

Day 5. Boaters who went into Hickling Broad will likely travel downriver from Ludham to Acle and on down the Bure, as did those who didn't go into Hickling Broad on Day 4. This night is likely best spent at some mooring around the Bure-Thurne confluence, perhaps at Thurne or in South Walsham Broad, or even a return up the Ant to the bridge or How Hill mooring. Boaters who plan to go into the South Broads, into the Yare and on to Reedham or St. Olaves return to the Bure and aim for the Acle vicinity for the night.

Day 6. This should be spent going upriver toward the starting point, exploring points of interest not visited on the downriver cruise. The night mooring should be at some spot within a few hours of the boatyard so that it can be reached by noon of the following day.

Day 7. For boaters who started at Wroxham or Horning and went directly downriver on Day 1, this is a good time to cruise on past the Wroxham Bridge into Coltishall, then back to the Wroxham, Belaugh or Horning boatyard.

For those who want to travel as far as possible during the week, forego the River Thurne and Hickling Broad and the waterways above the Potter Heigham Bridge, and strike out along the Bure for the South Broads Yacht Station in the heart of Norwich city (a twenty-four-hour round trip of cruising out of Wroxham). Or you may aim for Beccles at the upper end of the River Waveney (twenty-two hours round trip). Plan to cruise steadily outbound, then more leisurely on the return, stopping at the highlights as time permits.

Cruising Times: North Broads

The following times are for steady one-way cruising at an average speed of 5 mph. For a total time between extremes, add the legs. For example, cruising between Coltishall and the mouth of the Thurne takes 4½ hours.

Coltihall to Wroxham	1½ hrs
Wroxham to Horning	1½ hrs
Horning to Ant Mouth	1 hr
Ant Mouth to Thurne Mouth	½ hr
Thurne Mouth to Acle	½ hr
Acle to Stracey Arms	1 hr

Stracey Arms to Great Yarmouth	1½ hrs
North Broads—South Broads One-way:	
Wroxham to Reedham	8 hrs
Wroxham to Brundall	11 hrs
For the Rivers Ant and Thurne off the River Bure:	
Ant Mouth to Stalham (round trip)	4 hrs
Thurne Mouth—Potter Heigham (round trip)	1½ hrs
Thurne Mouth—Hickling Broad (round trip)	4 hrs

NORTH BROADS RENTAL BOAT COMPANY PROFILES

On the Upper River Bure: Wroxham/Hoveton is the boatyard town accessible by rail, but it is just a short run by taxi to Belaugh (2 miles/3 km by road) and Horning (5 miles/8 km). Unless you have rented a car, or are not otherwise dependent on rail, limit your choice from the fleets of the following companies. From the Blakes catalog: Barnes Brinkcraft, Brinkcraft Yachts (Sailing), Camelot Craft, Faircraft Loynes, Fineway Cruisers, King Line (Horning), Moores, Woods Dyke (Horning). In the Hoseasons catalog: Belaugh Boats, Brister Craft, Connoisseur Cruises, Royall & Son, Sabena Marine, Summercraft. Under New Horizon's flag, Horning Pleasurecraft at Horning is accessible, and New Horizon at Stalham will pick up in Wrotham (see profile).

On the Middle River Bure: Rail accessible boatyards at Acle are: Bridge Craft and Horizon Craft (New Horizon) and Anchorcraft (Blakes).

As we have stated, other than making recommendations to travelers from overseas who require rail service to and from London and other air gateways in Britain, we are reluctant to single out boat companies because, by and large, we find that they all operate fleets of clean and well-serviced cruisers. Nevertheless, besides being convenient to overseas travelers, there are some whose reception areas are above average, whose fleets are newer, and whose cruisers are exceptionally well-designed and fitted. But there are also others that offer less modern cruisers to persons and families on tight budgets, allowing vacationers of modest means to enjoy the waterways. For the best cruisers and best service there is, naturally, a price to pay. But after the cost and effort of coming all the way from North America, perhaps for a one and only journey on the waterways, the best values should be found. The following offer good values, and are convenient to rail. (H) = Hoseasons (B) = Blakes

For your convenience, agent contact information appears in Chapter 1 and is repeated at the end of this chapter.

- **Barnes-Brinkcraft Ltd. (B)**
  Riverside Road, Wroxham, Norfolk
  Tel: 1603-782625 Fax: 1603-784072
  E-mail: bookings@barnesbrinkcraft.demon.co.uk
  Website: www.norfolkbroads.com/barnesbrinkcraft

Owned and operated by the Thwaite family for thirty years, we found this to be a very progressive company based in a prime location just a five minute walk from the main street of town, making provisioning easy. A new reception center and headquarters were recently completed. There are nearly sixty cruisers in the fleet, of which twenty-five are 4-star standard. The layouts and interiors are designed and installed by the family, and have become refined over the years in part from listening to client suggestions, plus the good ideas and experience of the owners.

There is a wide selection, from small and economy (the 25 ft. Harmony class) to the large and luxurious 48 ft. Brinks Emperor with four double beds, and four single berths in six cabins. The price of the latter works out to about US $210 per person per week in peak season and about $150 in May and September ($110 earlier and later). That comes to $60 per couple per night in peak season, far less than a decent hotel room. This is not uncommon on the Broads. Among the sport cruisers, for two couples it is hard to beat the Brinks Contessa, and for two persons the little sedan cruiser Omega. The Duchess for one or two couples is an ideal, modestly-priced Broads cruiser, and we very much like Brinks Classic, a Blue Chip for two or three couples or a family. Most start days are Saturday, but other days are usually available.

- **Connoisseur Cruisers (H)**
  Wroxham, Norfolk
  Tel: 1603-782472 Fax: 1603-783089
  E-mail: info@connoisseurcruisers.co.uk
  Website: www.connoisseurcruisers.co.uk

A large company that manufactures top line cruisers as well as renting them. Although there is a fleet of nearly fifty cruisers at the boatyard just a hundred yards above the Wroxham Bridge, a principal market is the rivers of France, plus a small number of cruisers on Ireland's River Shannon (Lough Ree Cruisers, Glasson, near Athlone). The surprising thing is that the rental prices are so modest for cruisers of this high standard. In fact, on the smaller cruisers the company nets very little, due to the high ratio of the cost of manufacture and fitting to the amount they can be rented for. Thus, for boaters they are very good value.

Most of the cruisers are the Broads type, not sport cruisers, meaning maximum interior space and sliding roofs. A few of the larger models have dual helms, but typically they are forward, situated at the front of the salon area. There is a wide selection of sizes, ranging from the elegant and spacious GL2 which is perfect for two, to the very impressive C45, a 45-footer that comfortably sleeps six in a choice of either three double cabins or two doubles and two singles. Located on the Wroxam side of the bridge, a five minute walk from Roy's supermarket. The reception area is modest, but the cruisers and boatyard are impressive.

- **Belaugh Boats (H)**
  Belaugh (near Wroxham), Norwich
  Tel: 1603-782802
  Website: www.hoseasons.co.uk

The boatyard of this small, fourteen cruiser fleet, is forty minutes by river and five minutes by taxi up the Bure from the Wroxham Bridge. Such is the wandering of this lovely stretch of river, filled with birdlife, lined with trees, yet so close to town.

The company has been family-owned and operated for a dozen years which, given its small size, makes up with personal service what it lacks in selection of cruisers. The boats themselves are traditional Broads cruisers with sliding roofs; nothing very large, nothing very expensive. In sum, this is a modest operation, which in addition to its convenience to downtown Wroxham/Hoveton is why we give it special mention. It is ideal for travelers on a limited boating budget.

- **Faircraft Loynes (B)**
  Wroxham, Norfolk
  Tel: 1603-782207 Fax: 1603-784272
  E-mail: mail@broads.co.uk
  Website: www.broads.co.uk

Faircraft Loynes is part of the large Funnell Group Ltd. that, in addition to the Wroxham fleet of about thirty cruisers, also owns the substantial cruise operation called Herbert Woods based at Potter Heigham on the north River Thurne. It also has a center of very nice rental condominiums and cottages in Wroxham, plus rustic river cabins on the river at Horning, and wood bungalows at Potter Heigham. It also operates Broads Tours, offering a variety of itineraries.

The current company has combined several old-line companies: Loynes founded Loynes Boatyard in 1878, Woods founded Herbert Woods boatyard in 1928 and Charles Hannaford started Broads Tours in 1935.

The Wroxham boatyard sits next to the condominium

cluster at the south end of the Wroxham Bridge, three minutes walk from the town center and supermarket. The fleet overall is very nice and very well maintained, with a selection that goes from smaller inexpensive cruisers to the more elegant. Most are of sliding-roof Broads cruiser style with a choice of forward and center steering (we prefer the latter, with a better view from the helm), plus dual helm on some of the larger boats. They also offer four or five aft cockpit cruisers, most with folding canopy, which are fine for summer but should be avoided in possibly wet weather. For a couple, the Fair Contender is an inexpensive yet comfortable cruiser. For two couples or family of four, we like the Fair Courier of Fair Explorer. A bit older than the 1999 luxury class Fair Empress is the big Fair Princess that sleeps six comfortably, can easily be arranged for eight, and can even cram in eleven for anyone looking for low per person prices. Friday and Saturday start days are normal, but negotiate during off-seasons. Sailing yachts are also available.

- **King Line Cruisers (B)**
  Horning, (near Wroxham)
  Norfolk NR12 8PT
  Tel: 1692-630297 Fax: 1692-630498
  E-mail: kingline@norfolk-broads.co.uk
  Website: www.norfolk-broads.co.uk

This little fleet occupies a small part of a large marina at the lovely Broads village of Horning, about an hour cruising down the Bure from Wroxham (ten minutes by car). The boatyard and reception room are unpretentious—that is, not modern or spacious—but the owners and staff provide good service and offer a number of simple, very inexpensive cruisers as well as a few quite upscale models. The Calypso Queen class falls into this category. One of the neatest sliding-top cruisers we've seen among the smaller vessels is the Nevada King, and certainly one of the smallest with bow thrusters for maneuverability. It sleeps two comfortably, and two in a convertible berth in the salon. The Orlando King and Malibu King are two we can also recommend. They are almost twins in their design and layout, with berths for four and six respectively, or a version that has four doubles in three cabins plus the salon for family reunions or inexpensive per couple cruising.

Provisions can be brought from the supermarket at Wroxham if traveling to the boatyard by taxi, but there are also small grocers in Horning.

The other companies at Horning are Woods Dyke (B), Ferry Boatyard (B), Horning Pleasurecraft (H), and the small Norfolk Broads Yachting Co. (B).

- **Moores (B)**
  Wroxham, Norfolk
  Tel: 1603-783311 Fax: 1603-784295
  E-mail: traffic111@aol.com
  Website: www.boatingholidays.co.uk

This thirty-cruiser company caught our attention because of the good looks of its boats and the fact that all the crews we talked to liked them. Even the competition spoke highly of Moores. It's a family owned and operated company that has been in business since 1925. The boatyard is on the Wroxham (south) side of the Bure, a five-minute walk from the bridge and town center, and has four self-catering cottages in addition to the cruisers.

The Craigmore class sliding-roof Broads cruiser is an excellent inexpensive boat for two, as is the sportier aft-steering Aviemore, whose helm is high and dry, located inside. The Benmore is good for two couples or a family with double berths in two cabins, plus a convertible. The big 38-foot Merrymore sleeps six in two double berths and one convertible in the salon and in spite of its size the low hull allows passage under even the Potter Heigham Bridge (at low tide). Monday, Friday, and Saturday start days are available, but different for different cruisers.

• **New Horizon Holidays**
  The Staithe, Stalham
  Tel: 1692-582277 Fax: 1692-581522
  E-mail: info@newhorizonhols.com
  Website: www.newhorizonhols.com

New Horizon Group owns and operates the largest number of cruisers in Britain, some 670 in two boatyards on the Thames (see Chapter 3) as well as several on the North and South Broads. Founded in 1958 as Richardson Cruisers, the company now operates boatyards in Acle on the middle Bure (Horizon Craft), at Horning near Wroxham/Hoveton (Horning Pleasure-craft), at Norwich (Hearts Cruisers), and the main fleet of about 360 cruisers at Stalham. All the boatyards are easily accessible from a railroad station.

From this many cruisers there is never a problem in finding one that fits your requirements—only in choosing. The fleet, which now encompasses the former Stalham Pleasurecraft cruisers and two fleets on the Thames, is well illustrated in their substantial catalog. The boats run from tiny to very large, middle-aged to new, economy to luxury. We could, of course, inspect only a sampling of the cruisers, but those we saw appeared to be well maintained.

After receiving their brochure or the catalog, the best approach to booking at Stalham or any of their boatyards is to call or fax the main booking number shown above with a selection of two or three cruisers.

Stalham is at the north end of navigation of the River Ant, a good place from which to start a Broads cruise. There are grocers and other shops in the town, and although it is about twelve road miles from the railroad station at Wroxham, a telephone call to the reception office from the station or the supermarket or hotel will bring a vehicle to pick you up. The whole procedure is quite easy. If you'd like a week on the Broads and a week on the Thames, the company can handle it. The advantages to working with such a large company are selection and service (such as transport from the railroad station), and the versatility of having several boatyard locations to choose from. The disadvantage is that Stalham is a large and busy boatyard, rather hectic on main start days. This is best managed by planning to start on a day other than Saturday (the busiest), and by simply by departing Stalham to a quiet first night mooring downriver at Neatishead or Irstead.

In the US contact Great Trips Unlimited, Tel: 888-329-9720; www.gtunlimited.com

• **Royall & Son (H)**
  Riverside Rd., Wroxham/Hoveton
  Tel: 1603-782743 Fax: 1603-782743
Seventeen cruisers more or less occupy the boatyard of this family operation. A few are new, most are modern in style, and all are well maintained. Because of not being slick and new, some of the older cruisers offer large size for a very modest price. This is an unpretentious company that has been in business for a long time, and is well spoken of by its competitors. Very convenient, it is ¼ mile from the railroad station and town center.

The South Broads

Highlights
Unlike long rivers that lend themselves to linear one-way itineraries, the South Broads is an elliptical area, best to be circumnavigated, beginning and ending the journey at the same boatyard. Which one doesn't matter—just the most convenient. Like the face of a clock, the cruise can begin at the one o'clock point and return there, or start and end at the six o'clock position, or noon position. Thus, the only crucial

decision is to find the most suitable and convenient boat rental company. The later parts of this chapter define the starting points most convenient to travelers by rail, and highlights boat companies in those towns.

It is purely arbitrary that we start the highlights in the northwest of the South Broads at **Norwich**, then down the River Yare, past its confluence with the Haddiscoe New Cut and into Breydon Water, a semi-saline estuary it shares with the River Waveney.

There is no boatyard in the center of Norwich, just a long mooring along the River Wensum at a spot called **Norwich Yacht Station**, so boaters arrive from boatyards downriver at Thorpe, Brundall, Reedham, St. Olaves, and perhaps after three days cruising from Broads towns well to the north. There is a mooring fee of about £7 (U.S. $12) at the yacht station, but it is well worth it. From the quay walk across the Bishopsgate Bridge, then cross and walk five minutes with the high spire of the **Norwich Cathedral** as your guide. This will take you to the town center as well as to the magnificent Norman cathedral.

If arriving in Norwich a day or so before the start of cruising, en route to a boatyard in the vicinity (Thorpe, Brundall, Reedham), check Norwich Accommodations at www.s-h-systems.co.uk/norwich.html

Other accommodations include: Old Rectory (103 Yarmouth Road, Thorpe St. Andrew, Norwich, Tel: 1603-700772); Riverview Hotel, (25 Yarmouth Road, Thorpe St. Andrew, Norwich, Tel: 1603-431226); Station Hotel (5–7 Riverside Road, Norwich, Tel: 1603-611064, Fax: 1603-615161); Catton Old Hall (Lodge Lane, Norwich, Tel: 1603-419379, Fax: 1603-400339); Maid's Head Hotel (Tombland, Norwich; in US, contact Queens Moat Hotels, Tel: 800-641-0300, www.queensmoat.com).

The navigable Yare begins in the eastern outskirts of the city of Norwich where it is joined by its tributary, the

Wensum, which loses its name in the process. The Wensum is nevertheless important to boaters because it flows through the heart of the city, passing under its many bridges, ending its open waters at the **Norwich** mooring noted in the preceding paragraph. The length of the navigable Yare from Norwich eastward to its estuary, Breydon Water near the sea at Great Yarmouth, is an easy day cruise through flat countryside and low rolling hills, passing several pleasant inns and the towns of **Thorpe St. Andrew** (marina), **Brundall** (marina) and **Reedham** (marina).

At **Thorpe** the waterway divides around an island that came into being when the present main channel, called the **Thorpe New Cut**, was constructed to allow the passage of large vessels; the old channel, actually the Yare, creates a pleasant backwater where there are moorings and the boatyards Highcraft, Maiden Craft, Hearts Cruisers and Kingfisher Cruisers. This is the closest cruiser rental marina to Norwich, and a good starting point for traveling the South Broads, about a fifteen minute taxi ride from Norwich rail station.

Just west (upriver) of Reedham the **River Chet** flows into the Yare, and we recommend a diversion there, up the Chet about four miles to the village of **Loddon**. In fact, time allowing, we suggest that a day be devoted to the stretch between Norwich and Reedham with a detour up to **Loddon** and back, mooring at **The Archer's Reed-ham Ferry Inn** for the night. The inn, a grand traditional Broads pub, is a delight, and a place we recommend for dinner and ale, or at least a good pub lunch. The mooring itself is easy and the river slow; the only activity there besides the inn is the

Reedham Chain Ferry. It's the only chain ferry left in Britain, and perhaps in the western world. Simply put, the ferry connects the ends of highway B1140 by means of an iron barge equipped with a motor and drum that pulls itself across the Yare by means of a dangling chain between the banks. CAUTION: do not pass this point in the river when the ferry is operating.

Reedham is served by rail on the Norwich-Lowestoft and the Norwich-Great Yarmouth runs, with at least a dozen trains a day. It is a good beginning and end spot for an itinerary up the Yare and Wensum to Norwich, then back to head for either the North Broads, or the South Broads loop to Oulton Broad and on to the ancient market and garden city of Beccles.

If you want to arrive in the area a day before starting to cruise, but prefer to overnight near one of the boatyards rather than in the city of Norwich, ask the cruiser company about local accommodations, or contact: Braydeston House (The Street, Brundall, Tel: 1603-713123) or Riverside (Reedham, Tel: 1493-700054, Fax: 1493-700054).

A mile east (downriver) of Reedham the **Haddiscoe New Cut** joins the river, easily identified because it is a broad, straight, man-made canal about three miles long that connects the Yare with the River Waveney at St. Olaves to the south. Taking the cut saves three or four hours of cruising and may be useful at some point in your travels, but the journey along the Yare and the Waveney, which form a large "V" from where they converge and form the vast Breydon Water estuary, is worthwhile. Locals may say that it's a boring half-day along the "V" through miles of reeds, but it depends on what you're looking for. It is a stretch that supports outstanding birdlife, especially swans and the great marsh harriers, described above, who nest in the reeds, usually within a hundred yards of the rivers. One feeding encounter of a marsh harrier pair was, to us, worth the reedy route, but it is added to by a visit to the largest still-turning windmill in England, the **Berney Arms Mill**. There is good

mooring at the mill, which appears on the charts (on the north bank of the Yare, just west of where it becomes Breydon Water). The small museum inside the mill is interesting, and a climb up its many floors lays the expanse of the Broads at your feet. While there, birders should plan a walk or bicycle ride into the **Berney Marshes Nature Reserve** (information at the mill and from boatyards).

The River Waveney joins the Yare ten minutes downriver of the Berney Arms Mill, and together the two rivers become **Breydon Water,** a vast tidal expanse that supports a rich variety of birdlife. The basin makes for shallow water, especially at low tide, but the channel is well marked until it deepens again in the city of Great Yarmouth where the River Bure comes in from the North Broads. It, too, is a nature reserve, but from the water it is difficult to get into because of the shallow salt marshes.

At the juncture of the two rivers boaters can either continue ¾ hour down Breydon Water to **Great Yarmouth**, or turn south and around the bend into the River Waveney up toward St. Olaves and the end of Waveney navigation upriver of the town of **Beccles** (see The River Waveney, below). At the Great Yarmouth end of Breydon Water, the **River Bure** flows in from the north, marking a point of entry to the North Broads.

The navigable **River Chet** is short, running into the Yare fifteen minutes upstream of Reedham and ending after an hour cruising at the marinas at **Loddon**. It is a narrow river, shallow enough that larger cruisers with a draft exceeding 3½ feet should be very wary at low tide, especially in spring. It's best to ask at the Reedham boatyard if you have any doubts. Otherwise, the cruise is pleasant enough through the Hardley Flood Nature Reserve, and to the nice marina and the town. It is a good spot for an overnight mooring if time works out. The very old church of the **Holy Trinity** and the large graveyard that surrounds it are well worth the short walk to the market square, as is a look at the oldest alms box in England and the **Loddon Heritage Centre** housed in the church. Market day is Monday.

The **Waveney** is the other major river of the South Broads, and originates in the rolling hills of Suffolk and flows northeasterly to its confluence with the Yare which, as noted above, together form the vast estuary **Breydon Water**. It is navigable upriver for about an hour's cruising above the pretty market town of **Beccles**.

Beccles, where there are two rental cruiser boatyards, is a delightful spot to stay for a day, perhaps prior to departing onto the River Waveney and the Broads. It is at the southernmost end of the Broads waterways, and is served by rail from London via Ipswich, rather than Norwich, with trains out of Ipswich every two hours. There is an excellent public mooring, a Safeway supermarket nearby, and the town center is an easy walk. There is an interesting church, **St. Michael**, especially picturesque in that the bell tower stands beside the church rather than on top. There is a **Broads Authority Information Centre** at the quay. Boaters starting from a boatyard at Beccles usually cruise downstream, then return the last afternoon to pass by the boatyards and cruise another hour upriver to spend the last night at the mooring near the end of navigation. It's then easy to return your cruiser in the morning. (Because of narrow, swifter water and the low bridge, care should be exercised in going upriver beyond Beccles. See WARNING on the navigation chart).

Travelers wanting to arrive early and spend the night before the start of cruising can do so in Ipswich, or ask the boat company for recommendations in Beccles. Two good choices in Beccles are the Colville Arms Hotel, Lowestoft Road, Worlingham, Beccles, Suffolk (Tel: 1502-712571, Fax: 1502-712571) and the little Waveney House Hotel, just south of the bridge. There are private moorings at the latter, free for patrons who have taken a room or have dinner. (Check www.s-h-systems.co.uk/beccles.html for information.)

At its upper to central reaches the river winds slowly along reed and tree-lined banks behind which rise mixed marsh and forest (carr) that provide sanctuary for myriad forest birds and animals, while the river itself is inhabited mostly by ducks, geese, and grebes.

At mid-river, the **Waveney River Centre** lies along the north bank, complete with mooring, laundromat, and other boaters services. Ten minutes downstream a short canal (no locks) called the **Oulton Dyke** joins the Waveney. Bird watchers will especially want to take this, as it passes through the Carlton Marshes and the Oulton Marshes Nature Reserves and into the Oulton Broad. At the eastern reach of **Oulton Broad** is a major Yacht Station, complete with moorings, pubs, shops, restaurants, and access to supplies. The Broad itself, along the western suburbs of the city of **Lowestoft**, is populated, and is the only one where powerboat racing is allowed. Boatyards for two small cruiser companies, Hampton Boats and Topcraft Cruisers, are located there. As Oulton and Lowestoft are on the rail line, this is another convenient starting point for Broads exploration. For boaters from elsewhere, the trip from the Waveney along Oulton Dyke and Oulton Broad takes about two hours, plus any land exploration.

Downriver of the start of the Oulton Dyke is a small mooring from which **Somerleyton** and **Somerleyton Hall** can be reached. The village is an easy walk, as is the elegant yet homey manor house. Rebuilt in the 1840s, the house is the home of Lord Somerleyton, but is open to the public Sundays and Thursdays 12:30–5:30 from Easter to the 1st Sunday of

September, plus Tuesdays and Thursdays during July and August. This is a most exquisite house, rich in furnishings and art, set in expansive gardens complete with one of the famous English mazes. Lovely walks, and a good pub at riverside.

Past the quintessential Broads windpump called **Herringfleet Mill** on the east bank the **Haddiscoe New Cut** takes off from the Waveney, a constructed canal several miles in length that connects the Waveney with the Yare. Whether or not to take the Cut depends on whether or not you want to cruise on down the Waveney to Breydon Water, or hurry over to the Yare to start upstream toward Norwich. Most everyone who cruises the South Broads does, at one point or other, travel the Haddiscoe Cut.

At the juncture of the Cut and the Waveney lies the little village of **St. Olaves** (pronounced almost like "olives"). It is served by rail on the Norwich-Lowestoft route with several trains daily, and is an especially good start point for Broads exploration. This is partly because of its key location and partly because of the good service and excellent cruisers at the **Castle Craft** boatyard there. NOTE: Some of the through trains don't stop at small stations, so be sure to take one that stops at Haddiscoe. The village is little more than a cluster of houses, plus the remains of thirteenth century **St. Olaves Priory**.

Past St. Olaves, the Waveney almost stands still as it cuts through the **Fritton and Belton Marshes**, an hour cruising time where there is little to see except tall reeds, the distant Berney Arms Mill and a low hill along the south bank. The always present water birds include swans, moorhens, dabchicks, and migratory ducks and geese and, again, watch for the graceful marsh harriers. The first public marina is at **Burgh Castle**, just upriver of where the Waveney joins the Yare to form their estuary, **Breydon Water**. The ancient Burgh Castle is not what is expected—it was built well before the times of medieval castles. There are no high towers, turrets or crenelations, just massive walls firmly planted, probably forever, along the brow of a hill. It was known at the time of its construction by Romans in the third century as **Gariannonum**. It's a ten-minute walk from the mooring to the castle wall, and there is a half-hour elliptical walk around it, offering wonderful views across the Broads. There are marine services at the mooring.

The Waveney joins the Yare a few minutes cruising from Burgh Castle, and the wide Breydon Water stretches almost to the sea at **Great Yarmouth**. It is this point, the confluence of the Bure and Breydon Water at Great Yarmouth, where boaters decide whether to turn around and cruise up the Waveney or up the Yare, returning into the South Broads, or swing northward into the River Bure and on into the North Broads. As can be seen by this chapter, we suggest a week on the South Broads, or a week on the North, rather than a hurried attempt to see a little of both.

Itineraries

On our first Broads journey we began at St. Olaves (Rail station "Haddiscoe" on the Ipswich-Lowestoft line) and followed an itinerary that illustrates one of many approaches. We decided early on to spend the entire time in the South Broads, traveling slowly, stopping often, walking where possible. Had we wanted, a day spent going as far into the North Broads as Acle on the River Bure would not have been a strain, but we put it off to another time.

Day 1. Check out the cruiser, take instruction in the marina and on the Waveney, load luggage and groceries. Depart St. Olaves via the Haddiscoe New Cut for the River Yare and a first night mooring at The Archer's Reedham Ferry Inn. There is a small mooring fee if you don't eat or have a beverage, but the pub dinners and Norfolk ales are great.

Day 2. Take the Reedham Chain Ferry across, just for the experience. Cruise up the Yare to Thorpe St. Andrews, stop at one of the rental boatyards and shop for groceries. Cruise to Norwich Yacht Station, moor for the night.

Day 3. Walk to historic Norwich Cathedral and explore the

central city. Purchase a few groceries, if needed. If departing by noon, head downriver, then up the River Chet to Loddon for the night (5 hours); if later, plan on making Brundall (2 hours) or back to Reedham (4 hours).

Day 4. If the last night is spent in Brundall or Reedham, depart for Loddon. If the night was spent in Loddon, explore the village, visit St. Michaels. Depart early enough to make next night's mooring at Somerleyton Staithe (3 hours).

Day 5. Visit village and Somerleyton Hall and Gardens. Cruise up the Waveney for night mooring at Beccles (2 hours) or upriver of the Beccles Bridge (3 horus), stopping for breaks at moorings along the way. Explore Beccles, shops, buy groceries if needed.

Day 6. Depart early enough to cruise down the Oulton Dyke to Oulton Broad (2+ hours from Beccles), return to the Waveney, downstream past St. Olaves to Burgh Castle (4 hours). Moor for the night or, if time allows, go up the Yare to Berney Arms Mill (15 minutes) for a visit and/or overnight mooring.

Day 7. Return to the St. Olaves boatyard from night mooring at Burgh Castle, Berney Arms or Reedham by 9:00 AM.

This sample itinerary can be taken from any starting point along any of the South Broads rivers. For a week-long journey, a start at Thorpe St. Andrews, for example, suggests a first night mooring upriver in Norwich, then the itinerary can be followed much as the one described except one day earlier. Same with a start at Beccles, except that the boatyard staff will likely suggest as a good first night mooring Burgh St. Peter, then on down Oulton Dyke the following day. The variations are easy to work out and can be altered as you go, depending on how much time you spend walking the paths, visiting Somerleyton, Berney Arms Mill, and the like. The only two things to keep in mind: first, by mid-afternoon start thinking about the night mooring and, second, on the last night plan to moor within a short distance of your boatyard. Everything in-between is self-discovery.

For those who want to travel as far as possible during the week, it's possible to strike out from most South Broads boatyards for the North Broads and make the round trip to Wroxham on the Upper River Bure in a week-long voyage. It's approximately an 11-hour non-stop cruise between Norwich and Wroxham, for example, and 12 hours between Beccles in the south and Coltishall in the north. Boaters who want to take the fast pace should forego the side trip up the River Thurne and into Hickling Broad and the waterways above the Potter Heigham Bridge. Instead go up and down the Ant on the return leg from Wroxham and include a stop at Ranworth at Malthouse Broad. Alternatively, travel up the Thurne to Hickling Broad and forego the River Bure up to Wroxham. Plan to cruise steadily outbound, then more leisurely on the return, stopping at the highlight points as time permits.

Cruising Times

The following times are for steady non-stop cruising at an average speed of 5 mph. For a total time between extremes along a linear route, add the legs; for example, between Norwich & Beccles is 8 hours.

Downstream along the Yare:

Norwich Center to Thorpe	½ hr
Thrope to Brundall	1½ hrs
Brundall to Reedham	2 hrs
Reddham to Berney Arms	2 hrs
Berney Arms to Great Yarmouth	1 hr

Downstream along the Waveney & Haddiscoe New Cut:

Beccles to Oulton Dyke	2 hrs
Oulton Dyke to St. Olaves	1 hr
St. Olaves to Reedham	1 hr
St. Olaves to Great Yarmouth	2 hrs

Inter-waterway:

Beccles to Norwich Center	8 hrs
Norwich Center to Oulton Broad	6½ hrs
Beccles to Wrokham (North Broads)	11 hrs
Norwich to Wrokham (North)	11 hrs
Norwich to Stalham (North)	12 hrs

SOUTH BROADS RENTAL BOAT COMPANY PROFILES

On the River Yare: Rail accessible boatyards along the Yare are Reedham and Brundall. Also accessible is Thorpe St. Andrews, a ten-minute taxi trip from the Norwich railway station. Travelers without a vehicle wanting to start at a River Yare boatyard should limit their choice to the fleets of rental operators in those three towns. (H) = Hoseasons (B) = Blakes

In Brundall: Alexander Cruisers (H), Alpha Craft (H), Bees Boats (H), Broom Boats (B), Fen Craft (B), Freshwater Cruisers (B), Harbour Cruisers (B), Silverline Marine (H), Swan Craft (H), VIP Harvey Eastwood (B), Willow Cruisers (H)

In Reedham: Pearson Marine (H), Sanderson Marine (B)

In Thorpe (Norwich): Hearts Cruisers (H), Highcraft (B), Kingfisher Cruisers (B), Maiden Craft (H)

On the River Waveney and at Oulton Broad: Rail accessible boatyards are as follows:

In St. Olaves: Alpha Craft, Castle Craft, Norfolk Broads Yachting Co. (Sailing)

In Beccles: Aston Boats, A.E. Hipperson

In Lowestoft: Hampton Boats, Topcraft Cruisers

In Somerleyton: Crown Cruisers

- **Aston Boats Ltd (H)**
  Bridge Wharf, Beccles, Suffolk
  Tel: 1502-713960 Fax: 1502-711443

There are about twenty-three cruisers in the Aston fleet at Beccles and another fourteen at Loddon, a small town at the end of the short River Chet. As Beccles is on the River Waveney at the extreme south end of the South Broads, and because the boatyard is only a five-minute trip from the railroad station, this is an excellent starting choice for travelers without a car. There are many departures daily from London Liverpool Station to Ipswich, then by connecting train to Beccles on the Ipswich-Lowestoft run. Telephone from the Beccles railway station to be picked up.

Aston Boats is a partnership and has been in operation building and renting cruisers for some twenty-five years. Although a fleet of twenty-three isn't large, there is considerable variety among them, including a few older traditional styles as well as modern styles that feature more plastic and fiberglass and less wood and glass.

The boatyard is just across from the pretty public marina, and an easy walk from a Safeway for provisions. The first day should be spent moving downstream, with an ideal first night spent at one of the isolated moorings along the river or at Burgh St. Peter, just before the confluence of the Waveney with Oulton Dyke. On the last afternoon, return to Beccles, then spend about an hour cruising from the low bridge at Beccles upstream and moor for the final night.

- **Broom Boats Ltd. (B)**
  Brundall (near Norwich), Norfolk
  Tel: 1603-712334 Fax: 1603-714803
  E-mail: broom-boats@zoo.co.uk
  Website: www.broom-boats.co.uk/holiday

Broom Boats, in addition to operating an excellent fleet of some fifty cruisers, also designs, manufactures and sells them. Their cruisers can be seen in virtually all the waterways of Britain and Ireland, sporting a variety of rental boat company names and logos. The selection at Brundall is very good, ranging in size from two to nine berth, and in style from traditional sliding-top Broads cruisers to sporty aft-steering models for fair-weather cruising.

Their designs are the latest, and the innovations are hard to keep up with. Our favorites for two are the enclosed aft-steering Navigator class (which we enjoyed on the Shannon in Ireland with another boat company), and the sliding-roof Bosun. Their larger cruiser, the six-place Commander is excellent.

The boatyard is on the north shore of the River Yare, less than a ten minute walk from the railway station, with easy access to markets for provisioning. The start day is normally Saturday, but others are possible.

As the Norwich Yacht Station is only two hours cruising upriver from Brundall, a first night mooring there is ideal. There is a mooring fee of about £7 at the yacht station, but it is well worth it. Tie upriver as far as possible near the Bishopsgate Bridge, then cross the bridge for a five minute walk to Norwich Cathedral and the town center. Good cruisers, good service.

The Waterside Pub on the River Yare

- **Castle Craft (B)**
  Reeds Lane, St. Olaves, Norfolk
  Tel: 1493-488675
  E-mail: boats@blakes.co.uk.
  Website: www.blakes.co.uk

The cruisers of this small company, family owned and operated by Stuart and Christine Mendum, are among the nicest on the Broads. With a fleet of only eight, there are not many to choose from, but this also means that they are all beautifully maintained and immaculate—and with modest prices. We spent a few days on the Stirling Castle, a 34-foot sliding-roof Broads cruiser that sleeps four comfortably in two double cabins. We found it to be excellent, with plenty of room for two couples or a family. And the big 40-foot Pevensey Castle has space for six in three cabins plus a double sofa-bed, and three toilet/showers! There are three other classes in the fleet.

St. Olaves is a hamlet at the juncture of the Waveney and the Haddiscoe New Cut that connects the Waveney and the Yare, so it is an ideal start point for cruising the South Broads.

Transportation for travelers without a car is by rail from Norwich on the Norwich-Lowestoft run. There are many departures daily, but make sure to take one that stops at **Haddiscoe**. Telephone the boatyard to say which train you're taking and a car will be waiting (or phone after arrival and wait a few minutes). A grocery list is sent at the time of booking, so if you wish the first day's provisions will be on board. Then at your leisure, cruise northwest to Reedham, Brundall, or Thorpe, or southwest to Beccles where a large Safeway is near the mooring. There are also provisions at Oulton Broad.

Good and personal service, good cruisers, good location—and they know the territory well. Telephone the boatyard for advice and information; book direct or through Blakes.

- **Hampton Boats (H)**
  Oulton Broad, Lowestoft, Suffolk
  Tel: 1502-574896

Oulton Broad is at the extreme southeastern quarter of the South Broads, adjacent to the coastal city of Lowestoft. It is served by rail from London Liverpool Station to Ipswich, then by connecting train to Lowestoft. Be sure to take one of the departures that stop at Oulton Broad, just before Lowestoft station. Telephone the boatyard to be picked up. There are grocers within an easy walk.

Hampton Boats, founded in 1958, is family owned and operated, and builds its cruisers on Aqua Fiber hulls. Like others briefly profiled in this chapter, it is small, with a fleet of about ten cruisers, ranging from very little 25-footers (at very low rental prices) to a few larger that sleep up to eight. In general, the company offers economy cruising, and it is profiled partly for that reason and partly because of its accessibility and it proximity to grocers. It also makes for a good starting point for travelers who want to start their Broads exploration from the extreme south end of navigation.

- **Harbour Cruisers (B)**
  Riverside Estate, Brundall (near Norwich)
  Tel: 1603-712146
  E-mail: busterlayt@aol.com

Only nine cruisers comprise the fleet of this fifteen-year-old family operation, but except for a few they are all good looking, modern and well maintained. The oldest, Newlyn Harbour, is verging on the classic, a 40-foot craft that sleeps seven in four cabins, and four others in convertible lounges; the rental price is good for the size. For two people or a family of four we especially like the handsome Mullion Harbour and the Falmouth Harbour.

If desired, a grocery want list is provided at the time of booking and the provisions will be on board on arrival, or shop in Brundall. The boatyard is about 400 yards from the railway station on the Norwich-Brundall-Great Yarmouth line; Brundall is about twenty minutes by train from Norwich.

- **H.E. Hipperson Ltd. (H)**
  The Quay, Gillingham Dam, Beccles, Suffolk
  Tel: 1502-712166

Although the address is Suffolk, the boatyard of this small family operation is on the Norfolk County side of the River Waveney, close to the Beccles railroad station, to town and to the Safeway supermarket. We list the company because of its convenient access by rail from London, via Ipswich. On arrival, phone from the "call box" just outside the station and a car will be sent. There are only eight cruisers, and although most are older, they are well maintained and inexpensive to rent, especially the smaller ones.

- **Sanderson Marine Craft Ltd. (B)**
  Reedham, Norwich, Norfolk
  Tel: 1493-700242
  E-mail: colin@sanderson-marine.freeserve.co.uk
  Website: www.norfolkbroads.com/sandersonmarine

The family has owned and operated this small company since the late 1920s and knows the southern Broads very well. The fleet comprises only a dozen cruisers, none of them large or luxurious, and the reception area and boatyard are functional, but the location offers an interesting experience for travelers new to boating in Britain.

Reedham is a little riverside town just twenty minutes by rail from Norwich (well over a dozen train departures daily), and the station is one-half mile from the boatyard, so a nice itinerary is to travel from London to Norwich, spend the night, rail to Reedham (the company will provide transport from the station), then cruise upriver to re-visit Norwich from a mooring at the Norwich Yacht Station in the city center. Or a very pleasant approach is to spend the night before the cruise start day at a pub inn or B&B in

Reedham; this can be arranged at the time of booking.

The cruisers are of various designs and the rates are very reasonable. Two classes (Sand Eagle and Lady Sandra) are old-fashioned sliding-top Broads cruisers for four to six people, while the Sand Martin and Sand Storm (2 berth and 4 berth) are good economical aft-steering boats good for fair weather. Check the Blakes catalog for other styles, or talk with the Sandersons.

- **Silverline Marine (H)**
  Brundall (near Norwich), Norfolk
  Tel: 1603-712247 Fax: 1603-716990

A family owned and operated company since 1972, this fleet of some eighteen cruisers is characterized by a continual replacement program that assures that none of the boats are old and worn. In sum, the fleet is attractive and well maintained, with interiors that reflect the good taste of the company (they install their interiors at the boatyard). Among the smaller cruisers, the layout of the Silver Myth is especially spacious for two persons, and the Silver Eclipse for two couples or a family, but most of the other cruisers also exhibit good designs.

Brundall is twelve minutes by train from Norwich, and the boatyard is ten minutes from the Brundall station—just telephone the company on arrival and a car will be sent to meet you. A starting supply of groceries can be ordered at the time of booking, or can be purchased within a ten-minute walk of the boatyard.

Thorpe Green (Marina)
At Thorpe St. Andrews, Near Central Norwich:

- Hearts Cruisers (H)
  Riverside Road
  Tel: 1603-433666
  Main booking: 1962-582277

- Highcraft (B)
  Thorpe St. Andrews
  Tel: 1603-701701

- Kingfisher Cruisers (B)
  3a Bungalow Lane
  Tel: 1692-437682

- Maidencraft (H)
  Bungalow Lane
  Tel: 1603-435173

Except for Hearts Cruisers, now a part of the very large Horizons Holiday Group, these are small, old-line companies, mostly family owned and operated, each with fleets that include cruisers that range from modest to moderate luxury, with a few deluxe available, especially from Maidencraft and Kingfisher. They are noted here especially because they have the singular advantage of being in Thorpe St. Andrews, a suburb of Norwich city about fifteen minutes by taxi from the Norwich rail station and twenty minutes from the airport. As the most upriver marina on the Yare, Thorpe is a convenient start point for cruising the South Broads.

The best approach to finding the right boatyard among these, and booking the right cruiser, is through the Blakes and Hoseasons agency catalogs. As noted, the price is the same whether booked with the boatyard or through the UK agents. Groceries can be purchased at the supermarket in Thorpe, a ten-minute walk from the marina.

British Agents:

- Blakes Holidays Ltd.
  Tel: 1603-739400; Fax: 1603-782871
  E-mail: boats@blakes.co.uk
  Website: www.blakes.co.uk

- Hoseasons Holidays Ltd.
  Lowestoft, Suffolk NR32 3LT, England
  Tel: 1502-501010; Fax: 1502-586781
  E-mail: mail@hoseasons.co.uk
  Website: www.hoseasons.co.uk

North American Agents for Blakes:

- Great Trips Unlimited
  Tel: 888-329-9720; Fax: 503-297-5308
  E-mail: admin@gtunlimited.com
  Website: www.gtunlimited.com

- Blakes Vacations
  Tel: 800-628-8118; Fax: 847-244-8118
  E-mail: blakes1076@aol.com
  Website: www. blakesvacations.com

North American Agents for Hoseasons & Connoisseur:

- Jody Lexow Yacht Charters
  Tel: 800-662-2628; Fax: 401-845-8909
  E-mail: jlyc@edgenet.com
  Website: www.jodylexowyachtcharters.com

North American Agents for Connoisseur:

- Le Boat
  Tel: 800-922-0291
  E-mail: leboatinc@worldnet.att.net
  Website: www.leboat.com

CHAPTER 3

England: The Royal Thames

Visitors to England who know the Thames only as a wide and often turbid river may never have viewed it from west of Teddington Lock, near the London suburb of Richmond, where it ceases to be influenced by the sea. And, like all great rivers, its upper reaches bear little resemblance to its estuary. The long stretch of the "clearwater" Thames between the Lock westward some 125 miles into Gloucestershire is the Thames of old, tranquil beauty whose banks in part are lined with forests and isolated meadows, castles and towns, bridges and monuments, rowing clubs and yachting clubs, rich estates and little parks, abbeys, and palaces. The Crown's Home Park lines the river for a mile or so near Windsor where the Queen, we were told, can on occasion be seen by passing boaters as she strolls or rides.

Upstream past Windsor the river divides the towns of Marlow, Maidenhead, and Henley, flowing along the city of Reading, veering northward past Wallingford and Abingdon, and passes along the southern edges of Oxford, beyond where in olden times it was called the River Isis. It then meanders for many more miles until at Lechlade it becomes too small for hire cruiser navigation. It has passed near the Eton campus, Sinodun Hill, Buscot House and Park, and dozens of waterside hamlets, pubs, inns and shops.

In addition to this world of water, with its long periods of

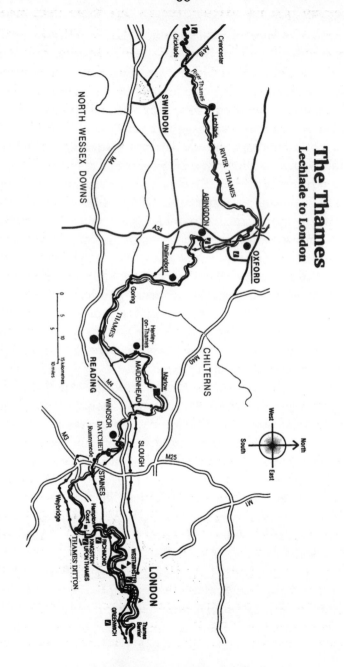

The Thames
Lechlade to London

The Waterways of Great Britain

undisturbed cruising and solitude, there are opportunities for walks along the riverbanks and through the woods. From convenient moorings it's easy to find paths that are well used, but still serene and quiet, inviting one to leave the boat to enjoy a change of view and atmosphere. Some walks may lead to areas alive with birdlife, and others into villages and to crossroads where a busy pub awaits your arrival for a local ale and a chance to vary your boater's diet. The most prominent of these many walks is the **Thames Path.** It runs for 180 miles (290 km) along virtually the entire length of the river from Trewsbury Mead, the official source, through London, ending at the Thames Barrier downriver of Greenwich.

The character of the countryside through which the navigable non-tidal Thames passes can reasonably be divided into three rather distinctive parts, all different enough from each other that boaters planning only a week on the river should decide in advance which two sections seem most appealing. This, in turn, will make clear the starting point for cruising.

• *Between Lechlade and Oxford:* Eastward from the extreme upriver (western) end of navigation and Oxford it is rural, tranquil and thinly populated. There are eleven locks, all with lockkeepers, that are smaller than the electro-hydraulic locks farther downstream. Most of the moorings are associated with the numerous pubs along the riverbank, although there are other small public moorings. Boaters on this stretch lean toward enjoying peaceful rural countryside and socializing at the waterside pubs. There are no grocery stores along the route between the two towns.

• *Between Oxford and Henley* are larger towns like Abingdon and Wallingford, with a short stretch of high population through Reading, attractive smaller towns like Goring and Sonning, and Henley itself, with appealing moorings just above the bridge. There are more private homes and more boats than along the western stretch, yet still much open space, forest and meadow. Between Goring and Henley the river passes through the Chiltern Hills where the scenery changes from the lowlands through which most of the Thames flows.

• *Between Henley and Kingston*, which is the at east end of navigation at Teddington Lock, the beauty remains but is slowly replaced by increasingly populous outskirts of London. The Henley-Windsor stretch is especially lovely, with many nice moorings, easy locks handled by lockkeepers, towns with easy access like Marlow, Windsor and little Datchet. As the river cuts through the increasingly populous areas and outskirts of west London, it seems to have been treated with a sense of pride and concern, and offers boaters considerable diversity of countryside, its environs graced by such places to stop and visit as Runnymeade, the Kennedy Memorial, and the great Hampton Court.

Wildlife of the Thames

Photographs of the Thames, anywhere from Kingston in the east to Cricklade in the west, would seem lacking if it were not for swans. Mute and whooper swans accompany boaters wherever they go, along with both resident and migratory Canada geese. Toward the western end of the river, where it is bordered by meadowlands there are more migratory species; and some, like the Egyptian and Greylag geese, rarely travel the North American flyways.

Lesser and great crested grebes arrive in late February and March, and by mid-autumn the eggs have hatched and most adults and young have departed. Other water birds that can be seen along the few marshy verges include Coots and Marsh Hens; Terns and Black Headed Gulls are common where the human population is sparse and, along with the more rare Kingfishers, seem also to like the waters around the weirs.

In spite of the prolific birdlife, the Thames seems to be of interest principally to boaters who want to see historic sites, visit towns, eat in pubs and inns, shop in villages, and picnic. Bird and wildlife lovers are more inclined to cruise the less heavily populated Norfolk Broads (chapter 2).

Highlights

In the other chapters of this guidebook that deal with rivers, the highlight overviews are taken in the direction of travel from the headwaters downriver toward the mouth or estuary. In the case of the Thames, however, the direction will be upriver because Heathrow and Gatwick airports, and therefore the most convenient starting-point boatyards, are toward the lower end.

These are short sketches of especially interesting or appealing places reasonably accessible to river moorings, intended to lead into a further look at a general guidebook to get the details.

Just upriver from the end of navigation at London's Teddington Lock and across the river from the Ferryline boatyard at Thames Ditton, several moorings along the north bank provide access to the Thames Path and the vast estate of **Hampton Court** and **Hampton Court Palace**. Built by Cardinal Wolsey, Archbishop of York, during the early sixteenth century, the palace is one of the most impressive of all the royal palaces, and came to the crown when offered by Wolsey to Henry VIII in an attempt to escape arrest for treason. Henry accepted the palace, the grounds and the employ of some 400 servants, but Wolsey was nevertheless dismissed and arrested. It is indeed an immense and magnificent place, so be prepared to spend much of a day to truly appreciate its history and the splendor of the palace and the gardens. The closest moorings to the West Gate are just below and just above the Hampton Court Bridge. Across the river the south bank is crowded with houses and areas of commerce. From Hampton Court the river winds through generally unexciting suburbs, punctuated by boatyards and an occasional glimpse of an off-river place of interest like the **Abbey at Laleham**, an otherwise unremarkable town that should be visited only if you have extra time.

Upriver of the commuter and boating town of **Staines**, in a parkland area of memorials, **Runnymede** is a reminder to all English speaking people that much of our own human history and values stems from here, with the signing of the **Magna Carta** in 1215. The site is recognized by a granite pillar, next to which is the **John F. Kennedy Memorial**, built on an acre of ground that was given to the American people by the people of Great Britain. Both memorials, as well as the **Commonwealth Air Forces Memorial**, perfectly exploit the lovely setting above the river. The entire area is owned by the Britain's **National Trust**, and the surrounding area and wooded slopes of Cooper's Hill provide a number of good walks, adding to its popularity for visitors. There is easy access from two moorings.

Old Windsor, just downriver from Windsor, has become the *burbs*, an expanse of housing that has obscured the old village and offers little incentive to stop. Just five minutes upriver from Old Windsor starts the New Cut, built in 1822 to provide a shortcut across a large river meander, which created **Ham Island**, now a bird sanctuary.

Next along the north bank is **Datchet**, with a quaint center retaining the sense of a village within the expanding London suburbs. It is easily accessible from London, and is one of the best starting points for a Thames cruise, since it is especially well positioned along the Thames for week long cruises along what we consider among the most appealing stretches (see Kris Cruisers). Across from Datchet, for a mile along the curving south bank lies the **Home Park**, the backyard of Windsor Palace, a broad expanse of open, grassy land with a tree-lined bank along the Thames, remarkably free of any sort of access control except for signs politely asking boaters not to moor. It's not the thing to trespass on Crown land, and one simply respects this.

A ten-minute train ride or half-hour cruise from Datchet,

Windsor and **Windsor Castle** are deservedly immensely popular places to visit. There are very nice moorings tucked behind a small island between the Windsor Pedestrian Bridge and the Elizabeth Bridge, both giving easy access to Windsor town. Windsor, the largest occupied castle in the world, dominates the busy village from the crown of a gentle slope, and is an easy walk from the riverside. The area around the castle is open daily, as are other parts of the castle at varying times. One can easily spend a half-day in the town, longer to tour the castle, and even a bit more to enjoy the walk across the Windsor Bridge into **Eton** and on up to the famous school.

From Windsor the river passes **Maidenhead,** a residential suburb, then along a beautiful stretch of palisade forested with beech and other deciduous trees, past **Clivedon House** high on a hill (now a $500 per night stately hotel) and **Cookham,** where from a mooring just above the bridge the village can be reached, a worthwhile walk to visit the town and the Wesleyan Chapel with its collection of the works of artist Stanley Spencer.

Marlow is a bustling Georgian town full of pubs, shops, grocery stores, a delicate suspension bridge, the Gothic Holy Trinity Church, and a tree-lined High Street, all easily reached from moorings below and above the Marlow Lock. The former is the more idyllic for an overnight stay, a bit away from the main population of boats in the upstream marina, but the second

Evening sky on the Thames at the Marlow Weir, Buckinghamshire

mooring above the bridge is also especially nice, situated across from a row of beautiful riverside homes. The £5.50 fee includes membership in the Court Garden leisure complex where there is indoor swimming, showers, and a cafe. On West Street, at the top of the High Street, in Albion House, Percy Bysshe Shelley wrote *Revolt to Islam* while his wife Mary Wollstonecraft Shelley wrote *Frankenstein*.

From Marlow the river wanders through pretty rural countryside, past the **Medmenham Abbey** ruin where from the mooring the little town can be reached, until just past the Hambledon Lock it becomes a three-mile long straight run to the Henley Bridge. This is the longest straight stretch of the river, and makes possible the famed Henley Regatta. The first Cambridge and Oxford boat race was run here in 1829, and the first Regatta was held ten years later and continues as a major event the *first week of July* each year. During that time **Henley**, a popular town year round, becomes especially packed and the river is closed to hire cruisers and other uninvolved power craft during most of the daylight hours. If planning a Thames cruise at this time, check with the rental boatyard about times, and plan to moor elsewhere. At other times, the long mooring upriver of the bridge is ideal, along a grassy public park, riverside walk, and weeping willows. The sign reads £6.50 fee payable at Town Hall (the domed building at the top of the High Street) but, better, wait for a fee collector. This is a delightful and manageable town to explore. If you decide to pay the mooring fee at the Town Hall, the pamphlet *Henley Heritage Trail* lays out a good walking itinerary. All services are available in town, and the walk to the moorings is only a few minutes. This is a good overnight stop, ideally Night 2 out of Datchet or, by pushing, out of Thames Ditton if the river isn't running fast; an easy Night 2 downstream out of Wallingford or Eynsham/Oxford.

Sonning is a very pretty and well preserved rural village an hour and a half up from Henley, with an easy and attractive mooring along the Home Park just upstream of the lock along the Thames Path. It's a short walk to the village church, cafe, pubs and shop and, in season, theater in the **Old Mill**. **Reading**, on the other hand, is a large industrial/university city that, although there are many points of interest, is difficult to manage from the river. There are, however, two cruiser boatyards there, Bridge Boats and Caversham Boat Services, as well as services along the waterfront. A visit to the **Abbey ruins**, the **Reading Gaol** made famous by Oscar Wilde in his *Ballad of the Reading Gaol*, and the two main museums are more easily accomplished on another stop.

The Thames course turns north at Reading, past **Mapledurham House**, which is worth a visit, but almost impossible to accomplish as it is open only from 2:30–5:00 PM on weekends and bank holidays and takes some other convolutions to get there. With a week to cruise, the time is better spent otherwise, such as a stop at **Goring**, half an hour upstream through Goring Gap, a stretch where the last ice age cut a channel through the chalk hills of the Chilterns. It is a delightful countryside, the grasses and beech forested slopes providing a change from the otherwise low lands that characterize most of the Thames Valley. The town is readily accessible from the moorings both above and below the lock, and is certainly worth a visit. Set in a wooded valley, the houses are mainly of flint and brick, and the intriguing riverside church contains one of the oldest bells in England, dating from 1290. Goring is a holiday destination and therefore offers all manner of shops and services.

Wallingford is a very old borough, having received its charter in 1155, and well worth a stop and a visit. From a mooring along the Thames Path upriver of the multi-arched Wallingford Bridge it's an easy stroll to the town center. Behind the George Hotel is the entrance to **Castle Gardens**, from which paths lead up the knoll to the ruins of an eleventh-century **Norman castle**. The hotel itself makes for a good meal stop and the eighteenth-century **St. Peter's Church** with its open spire is splendid. All services and supplies are available, and the boatyard of **Maidline Cruisers** is just downstream of the bridge. Wallingford is an excellent starting point for anyone who leans toward travel along the more rural, less populated end of the Thames, yet wants to include a visit to Oxford. It is about a week round-trip cruising time from Wallingford to the west end of navigation at Lechlade. A week-long round-trip downriver as far as Windsor is easily accomplished, but on to Hampton Court would require six days of six-hour non-stop cruising daily.

For three hours upstream cruising time (more when the river is high) the Thames cuts a number of sweeping curves and flows through countryside that varies from Little Wittenham Wood, to meadowland to low hills, and past a number of small towns like Benson, Dorchester and Clifton Hampden, but few public moorings. The city of **Abingdon** lies mostly along one bank, its center most easily reached from the mooring just downstream of the bridge, then back across the bridge. It's a busy market town, dating from the founding of an abbey some nine centuries ago, and is worth a visit to see the **Long Alley Almshouses**, the **Abingdon Museum** at the market place, **St. Helen's Church**, and to walk the old streets.

The complexity and size of **Oxford**, the splendid old university city makes it difficult to deal with from the vantage of a moored cruiser. The river itself skirts the central district and the Oxford Canal is not navigable by hire cruisers. This is not to say, however, that the town is inaccessible. The city's presence can be seen far downriver, and along its banks at the approach to Folly Bridge it is definitely an attractive urban scene, of terraced houses, and tall buildings and spires. There are a number of moorings downriver of the city's main center, but the best are along the south bank within sight of the **Folly Bridge**, a bustling social spot just west of Christ Church Meadow. There is a riverside pub there, and another mooring and pub ten minutes upriver between the **Osney Lock** and the **Osney Bridge**. Either are good spots to tie up, have a bite to eat and ask for directions to the **Christ Church Cathedral**, the canal-side towpath, and the central city. The Osney Lock is best for overnight, while the Osney Bridge mooring is best for daytime only. *SPECIAL NOTE:* Some of the larger cruisers, or those with high configuration, *cannot pass under the Folly Bridge*. Be sure to check with the boatyard.

Oxford University is comprised of thirty-nine colleges, the Museum of Modern Art, the Sheldonian Theatre, the Church of St. Mary the Virgin, Christ Church Picture Gallery, the oldest public museum in England, the remarkable Ashmolean Museum, the University Botanic Garden, and a central area packed with people and shops and restaurants, blending the old with the new. In sum, a week's stay in Oxford itself would be rich and full, so the amount of time you spend with a cruiser for a home base is a personal decision.

Thirty minutes cruising above the Osney Lock, the mooring at **Godstow Lock** is a good spot for an overnight stay, close to the **Trout Inn** on the weir stream and below the ruins of **Godstow Abbey**.

An alternative to making excursions from the river is to spend a day or two before or after cruising the river. At **Eynsham**, an hour or so along the great horseshoe turn upriver of the Osney Lock mooring, but only ten minutes by taxi from Oxford rail station, is the boatyard of **Red Line Cruisers.** This is the westernmost hire cruiser boatyard, and the location is a good starting point for boaters who want to make the three-day round trip cruise along the more isolated stretch of the Thames westward to Lechlade before sampling a few days downriver into Oxford, Abingdon, and Henley.

The thirty-five river miles from the **Eynsham** boatyard to the western end of hire cruiser navigation at **Lechlade** can best be characterized as tranquil, meandering and of smaller scale than downriver. That is, the locks are smaller, the towns are smaller, the river becomes smaller and the bridges are smaller, but the water meadows and wooded wetlands expand to provide habitat for birds and both migratory and resident waterfowl.

Just out of Eynsham the stretch is referred to as "the Wriggles," which soon straighten out as the river swings west through meadow and farm lands past the hamlets of Newbridge, Shifford, Radcot, and Kelmscot and many quiet moorings in between. This is an isolated part of the river valley, and there are no grocers as the villages are either too small or away from the river. There are, however, picnic areas popular with land-bound vacationers as well as cruise crews, and good pubs such as the **Trout Inn** at **Tadpole Bridge** and **The Swan Hotel** at **Radcot Bridge**. Fifteen minutes above the Radcot Bridge is **Grafton Lock**, perhaps the most remote-feeling of the Thames locks, then the tiny traditional village of Kelmscot with its fifteenth-century church and **Kelmscot Manor**, home of William Morris for many years, and of Dante Gabriel Rossetti for a time. The manor is open every Wednesday and in the afternoon of every third Saturday during spring and summer. The end of navigation for most power boats is at the Round House, where the unnavigable Thames & Severn Canal meets the Thames just beyond **Lechlade**. As the end (or start) of navigation, the town is river-focused and the riverside park is often full of people and the park mooring full of cruisers. The town center is easily spotted by the church spire, and the church is accessible from the river up Shelley's Walk. All needed services and provisions are available.

Itineraries

Because most boaters, British and Continental, drive their cars to the boatyards and return after the cruise to pick them up, at present there are no boatyards that offer one-way cruising. We anticipate, however, that as more foreign visitors catch on to the pleasures of cruising the waterways, and arrive with no plan to rent a car, this will change. Until then it means that regardless of the starting boatyard, all itineraries must be circular; that is, upriver and back, or downriver and back, or a bit up and a bit down. Thus, it takes at least two weeks to travel all of the navigable clear Thames, starting and ending at the same boatyard. In a cruise of that duration, carefully chosen towns and sites along the way can be seen at leisure and seen in considerable detail. On a one week itinerary, a section encompassing about half of the length can explored by choosing stops carefully, and with a bit of planning provides a most satisfactory and enriching glimpse of the Thames and the Thames environment.

The following are aimed especially at visitors from overseas for whom starting at the boatyards most convenient to Heathrow or Gatwick are the best. Day 1 assumes a mid-afternoon start after provisioning the cruiser and completing the necessary hands-on instruction. Refer to the previous *Highlights* section for short descriptions of the named mooring points, locks and towns, and refer to the *Rental Boat Company Profiles* later in the chapter for directions to the boatyard.

By dividing the river into three sections, a round trip along part or most of any contiguous pair can be covered in a week. The first itinerary covers roughly the central segment from Datchet or Runnymede to Abingdon. The second illustration runs between London at the eastward end of navigation and Wallingford, and the third starts at Oxford and goes upstream to the western end of navigation. It then turns and goes down as far as about Goring, or possibly Henley-on-Thames.

To the times noted in the following illustrations, add twenty minutes or so for each lock along the route, depending on how heavy the seasonal river traffic is.

Finally, such variables as river flow speeds, different lengths of daylight at different seasons, traffic at locks, and time spent on land along the way all affect itineraries. If you use one of the following sample itineraries as a basic idea, ask the boatyard staff what they think relative to the variables at the time of your cruise. The staff are there to help and advise, so talk to them about your general plans or get new ideas from them.

Day 1. From the Kris Cruisers marina at Datchet depart upstream and spend the night at the Windsor mooring; if full, either venture on to the mooring above Boveney Lock (20 minutes) or return to the small jetty adjacent to the Kris Cruisers Boatyard.

Day 2. Delay a visit to Windsor and Eton until the return (or take the train at Datchet for the ten-minute trip). From either Windsor or Datchet cruise to Marlow, spend a bit of time, and allow two hours to Henley-on-Thames to spend the night.

Day 3. Visit Henley, then proceed upriver past Sonning, allowing 4½ hours to reach the vicinity of Goring for the night, depending on the time, flow of the river, boat speed, and other variables. If you make it to Goring, it's possible to cruise as far as Abingdon before returning downriver.

Day 4. It is an easy run from Goring past Wallingford to as far as Abingdon (about 5 hours), but on the way up scout for a nice overnight mooring a little downriver of Abingdon. Start downriver to spend this night toward Clifton Hampden.

Day 5. It is about 5 hours of steady cruising downriver from Clifton Lock to Sonning, and 6 hours to Henley, either of them fine for the night mooring. Downriver speed is of course faster than up, but it's important to be in a position by now to be near the home boatyard by tomorrow night.

Day 6. Sonning to Romney Lock at Windsor is about 5 hours, Henley to Romney Lock is about 4 hours, so plan accordingly to be near Windsor this night in order to spend a little time in the town. Alternatively, it's possible, depending on river flow and on time of morning departure, to travel past Windsor and the Datchet boatyard as far as Runnymede (about 1½ hours below Windsor) for the night.

Day 7. Return by mid-morning to the Datchet boatyard from the Windsor area or Runnymede.

This itinerary again assumes a week on the water and includes the more populous east end of the river:

Day 1. Start at Ferryline Cruisers boatyard at Thames Ditton and spend the first night tied upriver at one of the moorings near Hampton Court, or possibly as far as Walton, but wait until the return to visit Hampton Court (or visit it from a land base before or after cruising).

Day 2. Cruise upriver, stop at Runnymede and visit Magna Carta Monument, the Kennedy Memorial, Cooper Hill, and the Air Forces Memorial. Continue upriver past Windsor toward night mooring between Boveney and Bray Lock.

Day 3. It is about 5 hours of steady cruising upriver past Marlow and Henley-on-Thames to the Sonning Lock for the night, but allow time for an afternoon stop at Henley and a visit to the town. Or, moor at Henley for the night, 1½ hours short of Sonning.

Day 4. Cruise toward Goring (about 4½ hours from Sonning) or, depending on the time of afternoon, on up to the one of the moorings as far as Wallingford (about another 1½ hours). In any event, plan to moor near Goring for the night.

Day 5. Turn and return downstream, aiming for the night at Marlow (about 5½ hours). Moor either above or below the lock and visit the town.

Day 6. Depart in time to arrive at Windsor (3 hours) before noon, and spend time in Windsor. Depart in time to moor overnight in the vicinity of Shepperton Lock (2½ hours) for the night, in order to return the cruiser the next day.

Day 7. Return the cruiser to the Thames Ditton boatyard by mid-morning. *If you want to visit Hampton Court from a cruiser mooring* instead of before or after the cruise, plan at least a half day, and consider making the upriver destination short of

111

Wallingford or even Goring, perhaps returning downriver from Sonning.

A good alternative to this itinerary can be taken in the reverse, starting at the Maidline Cruisers boatyard at Wallingford (easy rail access from London Paddington Station and from Gatwick Airport) and traveling downriver. Figure an easy week (30 cruising hours round trip) to and from Windsor with ample time to visit the town and Windsor Castle, Eton, Marlow, Henley and other spots along the way. A trip as far as Hampton Court is possible, but means pushing hard (36-hour round trip in good conditions).

This next itinerary again assumes a week on the water, and takes in the section from the vicinity of Goring/Reading up to the western end of navigation at Lechlade. *SPECIAL NOTE:* Some of the larger cruisers, or those with high configuration, *cannot pass under the Folly Bridge* in central Oxford. Be sure to check with the boatyard, especially any downriver of Oxford, if planning to pass the Folly Bridge.

Day 1. Bearing in mind that there are no grocery stores upriver until Lechlade (6–7 hours cruising), buy enough in Oxford or at the small store at the boatyard to last for several meals. Start at the Red Line Boatyard at Eynsham, just west of Oxford, and travel upriver to the first night mooring at either Bablock Hythe (1 hour/1 pub) or Newbridge (1½ hour/2 pubs).

Day 2. Cruise upriver to the end of navigation (about 4½ hours) and overnight at the Riverside Park at Lechlade (the *e* pronounced as in "stretch"). Visit the town, eighteenth century Buscot House and Park, shop for groceries as necessary.

Day 3. Early start downriver, steady cruising, past the home boatyard at Eynsham toward night mooring just upriver of the Godstow Lock near the nunnery ruins (about 7 hours). Avoid the temptation to go on to the Osney Bridge mooring where the mooring is excellent for daytime, but not for the night.

Day 4. Cruise a short distance (30 minutes) downstream and moor at Osney Bridge near Oxford center. Spend much of the day visiting Oxford. It is 2 hours down to Abingdon for the night, so plan accordingly; there are, however, several moorings before if Abingdon is not reached. *NOTE:* If you have spent time in Oxford from a land base, or plan to do so after the cruise, then this day can be spent cruising as far as Goring, which makes it possible to travel as far as Henley-on-Thames before returning upriver. But this requires careful planning and a pretty steady pace. Also, be aware of river flow speed that could slow your return appreciably.

Day 5. If last night was spent near Abingdon, it's about 9 hours of steady cruising between Abingdon and Henley, too far to go and then return to the Oxford area by night 6. Therefore, choose a nice night mooring upriver of Henley, such as Goring, and cruise easily, visiting Wallingford en route. *NOTE:* If the river is running fast (if you can't tell, this information is available at any lock or boatyard), then don't go as far as Goring, as it will be difficult to return to the Oxford area in time to return the cruiser.

Day 6. Return upriver at a moderate pace to reach night mooring at Folly Bridge in Oxford (about 6½–7½ hours), or on up to Godstow again if time allows.

Day 7. Return to the boatyard by mid morning.

Moorings

The following twenty-four hour Environment Agency free moorings are listed in the upriver direction from Teddington Lock near west London west to the end of navigation in Gloucestershire. In addition to these, there are numerous private moorings available for a modest fee, or free with patronage of the waterside inn, pub or restaurant, all marked on the navigation charts. Also, there is no reason not to tie up at any appealing spot that appears safe, deep enough, and not posted as private. In the cruiser there should be either a set of stakes to drive into a convenient bank or, as on the Norfolk Broads, a hook anchor, or simply securely tie the bow and stern to a handy tree or post.

Steven's Eyot below Kingston Bridge
Kingston Wharf, Kingston
Desborough Island (Old River)
Tow path at Weybridge opposite Shepperton Lock
Tow path at Dumsey Bend, between Chertsey & Shepperton
Tow path at Laelham Wharf
Tow paths below Staines Bridge
Tow path below Runnymede Pleasure Ground, Egham
Tow path above Boveney Lock (Windsor)
Tow path below Marlow Lock
Tow path at lower Lashbrook below Wargrave
Tow path above Sonning Lock
Tow path below Goring Bridge
Keen Edge Ferry, Shillingford
Tow path above Abingdon Lock
Tow path above Kennington Railway Bridge, near Iffley
Tow path at East Street, Oxford
Tow path upstream of The Ferryman Inn, Bablock Hythe
Tow path above Pinkhill Lock
Riverside at Lechlade

Best Times to Go

The winter months can be cold and dreary in England, so unless you are willing to accept gray weather in exchange for a relatively quiet river and low boat prices, we suggest not going before early April (but avoid Easter week). May to middle, or even late, June and again from early September to mid-October are optimum in terms of weather, fewer boats on the river, and fewer tourists in the streets, as well as lower prices for everything from motor cruisers and sailing yachts to restaurant meals. The summer peak period begins the last week of July and lasts until the end of August, so the Thames becomes quite crowded, especially from the London end near Hampton Court up to Oxford (a one-week-plus cruise). Also, avoid the *first week of July* in the vicinity of Henley where the Regatta, a major event each year, fills the moorings, and the river is closed to hire cruisers and other uninvolved power craft during most of the daylight hours. Plan to cruise and moor elsewhere.

Navigation

This is a very controlled river, with catch basins, weir gates, locks and the like assuring that there will be no flooding threat to valuable property along its course. The management of the waterway above the tidal Thames is under the Environment Agency, a shift from its former overseeing agency, the National Rivers Authority. The shift indicates a change in policy direction from commerce to tourism and the environment. The river is clean and its banks unlittered. Compared to many North American rivers, its flow is gentle, but even so a flood flow speed of five or six mph can slow a slow-going upstream-bound hire cruiser to a crawl. One late afternoon in a drenching rain we were approached by an Environment Agency River Inspector's boat with lights flashing. The skipper, replete in braided uniform and cap, hailed us and told us that the river was nearing flood stage and to moor at Marlow Lock and leave plenty of slack in the lines to allow the boat to rise with the river. At Marlow the water was almost level with the iron rings in the massive wood landing. We live on Oregon's Willamette River and know what flooding rivers are like, rising five or six feet or more in a few hours, so we heeded the warning and tied our lines high up the bank, one to a steel pipe post, one to a tree, and then carried the anchor up and jammed it among the tree roots.

We were prepared for at least a four-foot overnight rise. We didn't tie to the mooring rings because we figured they could be four feet under by morning. With that much slack the boat's fenders banged against the low wooden dock all night, but at least we knew we wouldn't be tipped under by tight lines and rising water. In the morning the mooring rings were indeed under water—about six inches of it, which meant that the Thames had crested there at something like two feet! The Marlow lockkeeper laughed good-naturedly when we told him of our efforts, and commented on the wild rivers of the American West.

If the river speed in flood makes cruising conditions at all risky, they "red sign" the locks, meaning no passage. At that point the hire boat companies send qualified members of their staff or other licensed people out along the river to meet their cruisers and pilot them home. There is a very complete communication system in place, creating a community all along the Thames.

"Gently Does It" is the theme of the Environment Agency. The speed limit is 5 mph over the river bed, a speed hard to estimate except by looking at the passing scene. The cruisers' diesels are governed at about 6 mph in still water, so at high water and fast flow it's possible to travel downstream at a "ground speed" of 12 mph and upstream at almost zero. If such conditions exist (rare from May to October), consult with the boatyard staff before finalizing an itinerary.

The navigation charts show most of what you need to know, from lock schematics to mooring points, but most do not show navigation markers. There are four colors of river markers to watch for:
• Two black spheres vertical on stake or buoy: Isolated Danger (Pass either side)
• Red & White Stripe: Isolated, normally visible, danger (Pass either side)
• Solid Red: Channel marker (Keep marker on port/left side cruising upstream)

- Solid Green: Channel marker (Keep on starboard/right side cruising upstream)

The position of the green and red channel markers are, of course, reversed when traveling downstream.

A booklet, *A User's Guide to the River Thames* published by the Environment Agency is very useful and available at no cost at all the locks and many of the boatyards. Also important is *Stanford's Map of the River Thames*, an essential navigation chart, which can be purchased for about £4.00 at booksellers and boatyards.

The Locks

To outsiders, there are a surprising number of locks on the Thames. Built over the decades to manage the river, each lock has a weir, or bypass, and the water flow is controlled by the lockkeeper through adjusting a number of gates, in effect more or less damming the river. For boaters the weirs are roaring waterfalls adjacent to each lock, wide but not very high, and are to be kept clear of. The locks themselves, on the other hand, are often social spots where boaters of many nationalities chat with each other and the keeper while cruisers, sailing yachts, rowing shells and the occasional tourist steamer together rise or fall in the lock chamber. Unlike most locks on the canals, all forty-three of the Thames locks between Teddington Lock in London and St. John's Lock in Lechlade are operated by a keeper. Given that on a week-long cruise slightly less than two-thirds of the river is normally covered, this means passing through twenty-eight locks. Four a day, each taking from fifteen minutes to a half-hour, means between one and two hours a day are devoted to lock passage. This, we found, was a pleasant diversion, each lock having its own "personality" and providing an opportunity to stroll around.

Two people on a cruiser are the minimum crew. The procedure is simple: when the lock gates open, proceed in at the

lowest speed possible consistent with maintaining steering—
that is, keep power, do not coast, using the forward/reverse lever
to control speed. Obey the instructions of the lockkeeper. The
other crew member tosses the bow line and stern line to the
keeper who passes it once loosely around the bollard or cleat on
the lock side and drops the line end back to be held by one or
two crew members as the boat slowly rises or falls. A couple can
easily accomplish this; the skipper simply cuts power when one
of the lines is passed, steps out and tosses the other line.

There are always moorings above and below a lock, many
of them very attractive and ideal for the night.

Although most cruiser rental companies do not rent boats
between late-October and mid-March, the locks operate year
around.

November—March	9:15 AM–4:00 PM
April	9:00 AM–5:30 PM
May	9:00 AM–6:30 PM
June—August	9:00 AM–7:00 PM
September	9:00 AM–6:00 PM
October	9:00 AM–5:00 PM

Cruising Times

With all the monuments, parks, and towns to explore, the pubs
and restaurants to enjoy, the pauses for photography, the picnics,
figure a week for a round trip from any starting-returning point.
In general we recommend making the best time going and a
slower return, noting places and sites outbound where you want
to stop later. In this way of pacing yourself, there will be no need
to worry about missing a particular site because of a final rush to
return the boat. Plan to spend the last night moored within a
few hours of your home base.

Assuming no stops and maximum cruising speed,
following are the approximate one-way cruise times in hours
between key points along the Thames from the west at
Lechlade downstream to Teddington Lock near London.

Times assume an average speed of 5 mph over the riverbed. To these times, add twenty minutes per lock (refer to the navigation chart for number of locks).

Lechlade to Eynsham	6 hrs
Eynsham to Oxford (Osney Bridge)	1½ hrs
Osney Lock to Abington	2 hrs
Abington to Wallingford	3 hrs
Wallingford to Goring	1½ hrs
Goring to Reading	2½ hrs
Reading to Sonning	½ hr
Sonning to Henley	1½ hrs
Henley to Marlow	1½ hrs
Marlow to Windsor	3 hrs
Windsor to Datchet Village	½ hr
Datchet to Runnymede Memorial	½ hr
Runnymede to Hampton Court	3½ hrs
Hampton Court to Thames Ditton	½ hr
Teddington to End of Navigation	½ hr

Getting There

An economic advantage of cruising, as has been noted, is that there is no need to rent a car simply to have it stand unused at the boatyard for a week or more. Although the directions to each of the cruiser companies are described in the following profiles, in general the best way of traveling from Heathrow International is by taxi (or other hire company as noted in the profiles) to the boatyards of the lower Thames, specifically at Datchet and Thames Ditton. For the boatyards in Wallingford and Eynsham, the best way is by rail.

From Gatwick, the taxi fare would be far too much to make it feasible, even to the lower Thames boatyards, so we recommend rail. There are trains every fifteen minutes or so between Gatwick and London's Victoria Station, but there are no direct rail connections from Gatwick to the boatyard towns.

Travelers into Gatwick should consider arriving early and spending a day or two in London rather than adding hours of ground transportation to a long overseas flight. Take the train to the boatyard town the following day and arrive rested and ready to cruise.

We have profiled no boatyards difficult to get to, although a short taxi trip might be necessary from the railroad.

Choosing a Boat Company

Reading the Overview and the Highlights summaries at the beginning of this chapter, along with materials from the British Tourist Authority and more general travel guides, all joined with your personal inclinations, will help you first reach the decision of where to start your cruise. This will limit your search. Besides that, we have considered the following criteria, all of which make cruising more convenient for overseas visitors:

—Convenient to destination airports.

—Located in or near population centers where there are lodgings, pubs, and restaurants and, importantly, an adequate grocery store within easy walking distance of the marina (or one that will deliver or fill orders placed with the boat company).

—Located in spots from which the most interesting itineraries can be carried out.

—A good selection of cruisers, well-maintained fleet, fair prices, and the ability to provide full support and service to their clients.

The fleets of the selected boatyards comprise over 120 rental cruisers of all sizes, styles, and configurations, ample to cover the needs of all who book appropriately in advance. The other cruiser hire companies are listed but not profiled.

RENTAL BOAT COMPANY PROFILES

All telephone and fax prefixes from the US are 011-44 (+ the number listed); when calling within the UK, add "0" before the number. Additional general information can be obtained by contacting The Thames Hire Cruiser Association, Ash Island, Hampton Court, Surrey, KT8 9AN, Tel: 1819-791997.

For convenience, agent information appears in Chapter 1 and is repeated at the end of this chapter.

- **Kris Cruisers**
  Southlea Road, Datchet
  Berkshire SL3 9BU
  Tel: 1753-543930 Fax: 1753-584866
  E-mail: sales@kriscruisers.co.uk
  Website: www.kriscruisers.co.uk/cruisers

We like this company for several reasons: a good selection of cruisers from a fleet of about two dozen, a boatyard in a lovely setting across from the royal Home Park at Windsor, close to Heathrow, convenient to London by rail, and an excellent starting point for cruising. The family owner-operators, the Clarks, have been in operation since Chris Clark founded the boatyard some thirty-five years ago and truly know the business and the river. The center of Datchet is two blocks from the small marina and, except for being in the flight pattern for Heathrow, it still feels like a rural village.

Among the cruisers, the small, new Lady Chloe is fine for two people in good weather, but as it is a sport sedan with folding canopy it is not the best choice if it rains; for a modest price small cruiser we suggest the slightly larger, slightly older Lady Karen, or the older traditional design, Lady Keeleigh. Among the larger cruisers, we like both the Lady Diana and the Lady Pamela, both easily sleeping six but crowded for eight. The 43-foot Lady Selina is their sliding-top luxury cruiser for six.

Provisioning can be handled at any of several small grocers in Datchet, or buy enough for a few meals and shop again upriver at Marlow or in the supermarket at Henley-on-Thames.

Getting to the boatyard without a rental car is not a problem. If going directly from Heathrow, take either a regular taxi or, much better, telephone Station Cars at 01753-545000, 955000, or 681000 on arrival. They have an arrangement with Kris Cruisers and will pick up at the baggage terminal. The price of under £15 from Heathrow is about a third that of a regular taxi fare, and the trip time is twenty minutes to the boatyard. From far more distant Gatwick the price of a taxi would be prohibitive, so take the express train to London Victoria Station (about four trains an hour), then taxi, bus or tube to Waterloo Station. All departures to Datchet are from London Waterloo station; take the London-Windsor train and get off at Datchet, the next to last stop, about 45 minutes travel time from central London. There are two to four departures per hour and the fare is about £6. From the rail stop at Datchet, it is a two-minute downhill walk to the Thames and the Kris boatyard.

If not planning a visit to London before the start of cruising, an ideal approach is to arrive in Datchet a day or two early and visit Windsor and Eton, a ten-minute rail trip away. For overnight, we recommend a stay at *The Manor Hotel* in central Datchet, a two-minute walk from the rail stop and four minutes from the boatyard (Tel: 1753-543442; Fax: 1753-545292; Website: www.smoothhound.co.uk/hotels/manorc.) Book well in advance. Or stay at *The Chimneys*, a very nice inn (Tel: 1753-580401; Fax: 1753-540233; E-mail: the-chimneys @smsemail.force9.co.uk).

Ideal first night moorings are upriver at Windsor or the Boveney Lock (½ hour), or downriver at Runnymede (½ hour). See the first sample itinerary for one possibility, but also consider starting downriver to visit Runnymede and Hampton Court, then not cruising as far upriver.

Boats are available for starts on several days, depending on the season, so ask before booking to suit your travel plans.

For brochures, information and booking: Contact Kris Cruisers direct, check their website, or contact an agent for a brochure. The prices are the same except that Kris charges a 1% fee for credit card payment. As the latter of the two US agents may charge a higher fee, compare prices between the two US agents.

UK agent: Blakes Holiday Boating, US agents: Great Trips Unlimited or Blakes Vacations. See agent information at the end of this chapter.

- **Ferryline Cruisers**
  Ferry Yacht Station, Ferry Road
  Thames Ditton, Surrey KT7 0YB
  Tel: 208-398-0271 (Main Tel: 1692-582277)
  Fax: 1692-581522
  E-mail: info@newhorizonhols.com
  Website: www.newhorizonhols.com
  Also: www.holidayuk.co.uk/afloat/newhorizon/index.htm

This is one of two boatyards on the Thames, the other at Wallingford (see below), that have been independently owned and operated for many years. They were acquired several years ago by New Horizon Group, a company that owns and operates the largest number of cruisers in Britain, some 670 total in the two Thames boatyards and several on the North and South Broads. There are about 45 cruisers in each of the two Thames fleets, ranging from small, older, simple, economy-priced boats to a few large and very elegant ones, plus several very nice small craft. Ideal for a couple or family of four is the classy 35-foot, two-helm M.C. Prisma, at a naturally higher price. For a larger (sleeps four to six) moderate price cruiser the Miss Selina and Miss Olive are good. The 50-foot Miss Sheridan is the largest cruiser on the Thames, sleeps eight in four cabins, and up to twelve with two extending berths in the salons. It's also the least expensive per person. With the relatively new ownership we suspect that the fleet will be in a state of flux as new cruisers are added and older ones are sold off. We suggest getting their latest brochure or catalog, and also talking with boatyard staff for their recommendations.

Although the boatyard is very convenient to Heathrow (and central London by rail), Thames Ditton is densely populated and the reception office and marina are at the end of a long rather narrow street. Which is only to say that, unlike Datchet, Wallingford, and Eynsham, this is not a particularly attractive area to spend much time in prior to the cruising start day. If arriving in England a day or so early, rest up elsewhere and travel to the boatyard on the start day. If you don't have a car, discuss provisioning with the boatyard staff at the time of booking. Although there are grocers in the vicinity, just buy enough for a few meals and plan to shop upriver at Datchet, Windsor, or Marlow.

Getting to the boatyard from Heathrow is best by taxi and should not exceed £30–35; tell the driver "Ferry Yacht Station, Ferry Road, Thames Ditton." From central London, or arrivals at Gatwick via central London, rail service is frequent out of Victoria Station to the overground station at Surbiton (via Clapham Junction), then by taxi for the short journey to the boatyard. By car, look for the A307 and follow the map.

Ideal first night moorings after a mid-afternoon start are downriver about an hour to Teddington Lock or, if planning a mainly upriver cruise, pass by Hampton Court and test your skills on two easy locks en route to a mooring at Walton. Refer to the second sample itinerary for a good approach. Boats are available for starts on Monday, Friday or Saturday, with weekend or mid-week short breaks on some cruisers.

For brochures, information and booking: contact the main office number shown above and ask for the brochure. After looking them over, if you have questions about specific cruisers or the Thames, call the boatyard. For booking at Thames Ditton, Wallingford, or any of the New Horizons boatyards, call or fax the main booking number with a selection of two or three cruisers. This central office can deal with most questions as well as making your booking. Or, contact the US agent Great Trips Unlimited, Tel: 888-329-9720; Fax: 503-297-5308; E-mail: admin@qtunlimited.com; Website: www. qtunlimited.com

- **Maidline Cruisers**
  Chalmore Meadow, St. Lucians Lane
  Wallingford, Oxfordshire OX10 9EP
  Tel: Boatyard 1491-836088; Main Tel: 1692-582277
  Fax: 1692-581522
  E-mail: info@newhorizonhols.com
  Website: www.holidayuk.co.uk/afloat/newhorizon/index.htm

Maidline is the other long-time independent operator that has been acquired by the very large New Horizons Group based in Stalham in the Norfolk Broads. The boatyard is included here in part because of its location just above mid-way on the Thames, allowing for week-long itineraries upriver as far as Oxford and down as far as Henley-on-Thames. It is also included because it is convenient to London and Oxford, and has a good selection of cruisers and an experienced manager.

The fleet of some 45 cruisers offers a wide selection and, as part of the same company, is similar to that described above in the Ferryline Cruisers profile. The New Horizon brochure and catalog show pages of illustrations of a combined fleet, designating which cruiser is based at each of the two locations.

Wallingford is an attractive old town, its downtown streets sometimes crowded with cars, but comfortable for an early arrival before the cruising start day, where time can be spent at the Wallingford Museum, St. Peter's Church, and the Castle Garden and Norman castle behind the George Hotel: For overnight, book a room at the George on High Street (Tel: 1491-836665 or ask the boatyard staff to book for you).

There are grocers nearby so provisioning is not a problem.

The boatyard is a five-minute walk downriver of the town center and bridge.

There is rail service from central London Paddington Station on the London-Reading-Didcot Parkway-Swansea route; stop at Didcot Parkway and take a taxi eight miles to the boatyard or central Wallingford. There is also bus service from Gatwick to Oxford via Wallingford, and between Heathrow and Maidenhead-Henley-Wallingford-Abingdon-Oxford (Thames Transit and Oxford City Line). Telephone the boatyard from the phone box at the bus station and they will come for you. Ask questions of the local boatyard staff, not the main office switchboard in Norfolk, about transportation specifics. Inquire if Cholsey is the better rail stop at the time. By car, Wallingford is just off the A423 Oxford to Maidenhead road with easy access to the M4 and M40 motorways.

A nice first night mooring downriver is at Goring (1½ hours), and upriver at any of the moorings along the Thames Path up to around Clifton Hampton.

For brochures, information and booking: contact the main office number shown above and ask for the catalog. Follow the same procedures as in the last profile (Ferryline Cruisers).

• **Red Line Cruisers (Oxford)**
Eynsham, Oxon OX8 1DA
Tel: 1865-882542 Fax: 1865-880056
E-mail: red-line@compuserve.com

Red Line offers a small assortment of cruisers from a very good location for exploring the upper Thames (also named the River Isis upstream of here), as well as the Oxford area and as far down river as around Reading. Or, if all cruising is downriver, as far as Henley, Marlow, and Maidenhead—a round trip to Windsor requires steady cruising and few stops. The fleet also includes five narrowboats as Eynsham is a gateway to the Oxford and Grand Union Canals.

The boats are for the most part older models, but comfortable and well maintained. The three smaller two-to-four-person cruisers are sport type with folding canopy over the cockpit and steering position, which is great for summer cruising, but not the best if you are planning to travel before late May or after early September. For these off-season times the best bets are the odd little Red Deer for economy or, much better, the more spacious Red Queen. In fact, for a modest amount more consider the Red Coral, a 34-foot sliding-top cruiser that comfortably sleeps four in two cabins. The choice isn't great, but owner Michael Peck is very helpful and, as noted, the location is very good.

Without a rental car, getting to the boatyard is a matter of getting to Oxford. There are many trains daily from central London Paddington Station to Oxford; from the Oxford railway station call a taxi for the twenty-minute, £10 trip. There is also bus service from Gatwick to Oxford, and between Heathrow and Oxford (Oxford City Line; Thames Transit bus line).

If driving and you happen to pass by a market in Oxford, stock up there; otherwise, rely on the limited but short-term grocery supply at the little store at the boatyard, buying enough for a few meals to begin the cruise. There are, however, no grocers (only pubs and inns for meals) upriver until Lechlade, 1½ days away, where groceries are plentiful.

If you plan to arrive early or stay after the cruise, there are many hotels in Oxford, among them the excellent Old Parsonage Hotel at 1 Banbury Road (Tel: 1865-310210; Fax: 1865-311262; E-mail: oldparsonage@dial.pipex.com); also, the inexpensive Swinford Park is not in central Oxford but closer to the boatyard at Swinford Park, Eynsham (Tel: 1865-881212); modern in Oxford is the Oxford Moat House Hotel (Tel: 1865-489988; Fax: 1865-310259). The old, traditional Mitre on the High Street is another choice (Tel: 1865-244563). Or look at the selections on the internet at http://www.s-h-systems.co.uk/oxford.html.

Contact the UK agent or the US agents for the Blakes catalog; after selecting two or three possible cruisers either contact the boatyard directly or book through one of the agents. There is no price difference (but compare prices between the two US companies).

UK Boat agent: Blakes Holiday Boating. US agents: Great Trips Unlimited or Blakes Vacations. See agent information at the end of this chapter.

• **Temple Cruisers**
  John and Sharon Davies
  Tel: Staines 1784-453433
  Website: www.cuddly.demon.co.uk/temple/temple.htm
We have not visited this boatyard or looked at their fleet, but include it because Staines is an ideal starting point on the lower Thames near Heathrow, lying along the river just down from Datchet and Runnymeade. It is an independent that describes itself as follows:

Temple Cruisers is a small family-run hire company, offering distinctive motor cruisers for hire on the River Thames. The cruisers look like privately-owned cruisers as they do not carry any advertising insignia. Full tuition (instruction) and practice can be provided and inspections are welcome.

A short break of 3 days can be from around £130 to £225, depending on season. Prices for one week range from £210 to £395.

The company policy is to maintain quality motor cruisers in excellent condition and offer them for hire at competitive rates. They believe that if you are proud of the cruiser you have hired, you will treat it with care and consideration and thus enable the standards and pricing to be maintained. Rent a private four-to-six berth quality cruiser and enjoy the good life cruising the Royal Thames in a motor cruiser you would be proud to own.

Ask the boatyard about transportation, but it should be a simple matter of taking a taxi from Heathrow.

British Agents:
- Blakes Holidays Ltd.
  Tel: 1603-739400; Fax: 1603-782871
  E-mail: boats@blakes.co.uk
  Website: www.blakes.co.uk

- Hoseasons Holidays Ltd.
  Lowestoft, Suffolk NR32 3LT, England
  Tel: 1502-501010; Fax: 1502-586781
  E-mail: mail@hoseasons.co.uk
  Website: www.hoseasons.co.uk

North American Agents for Blakes:
- Great Trips Unlimited
  Tel: 888-329-9720; Fax: 503-297-5308
  E-mail: admin@gtunlimited.com
  Website: www.gtunlimited.com

- Blakes Vacations
  Tel: 800-628-8118; Fax: 847-244-8118
  E-mail: blakes1076@aol.com
  Website: www. blakesvacations.com

North American Agents for Hoseasons & Connoisseur:
- Jody Lexow Yacht Charters
  Tel: 800-662-2628; Fax: 401-845-8909
  E-mail: jlyc@edgenet.com
  Website: www.jodylexowyachtcharters.com

North American Agents for Connoisseur:
- Le Boat
  Tel: 800-922-0291
  E-mail: leboatinc@worldnet.att.net
  Website: www.leboat.com

CHAPTER 4

England: Lake Windermere

In the northeast of England where the country is at its narrowest, not far from the border with Scotland, lies the county of Cumbria and the Lake District. At its southern center lies England's largest lake, Windermere. Surrounded by a number of lesser but equally beautiful lakes nestled in the hills of the Lake District National Park, and bordered along its dozen-mile-long eastern shore by small towns and hamlets, marinas, shops, parks, hotels, resorts, trails, roads, manor houses and smaller estates, the Lake Windermere area is one of the most popular vacation destinations in Britain, for both British and foreigners.

Beautiful and appealing? Yes. But not at peak tourist season, school holidays or bank holidays, and even rarely on weekends when the weather is decent. Parking at the best of times is difficult, at the worst of times, impossible. Crowds swarm the picturesque streets of the lakeside villages of Bowness, Ambleside, and Windermere, and the number of stores and restaurants and hotels and guest houses is astounding. Yet in spite of all this, people continue to come, lured by the still untrammelled, tranquil beauty of the mountains that comprise many square miles of countryside just a short distance from the often packed streets of the towns. It is these hills and lakes, and the then peaceful villages that drew from Wordsworth words such as, "—the loveliest spot that man hath ever found,"

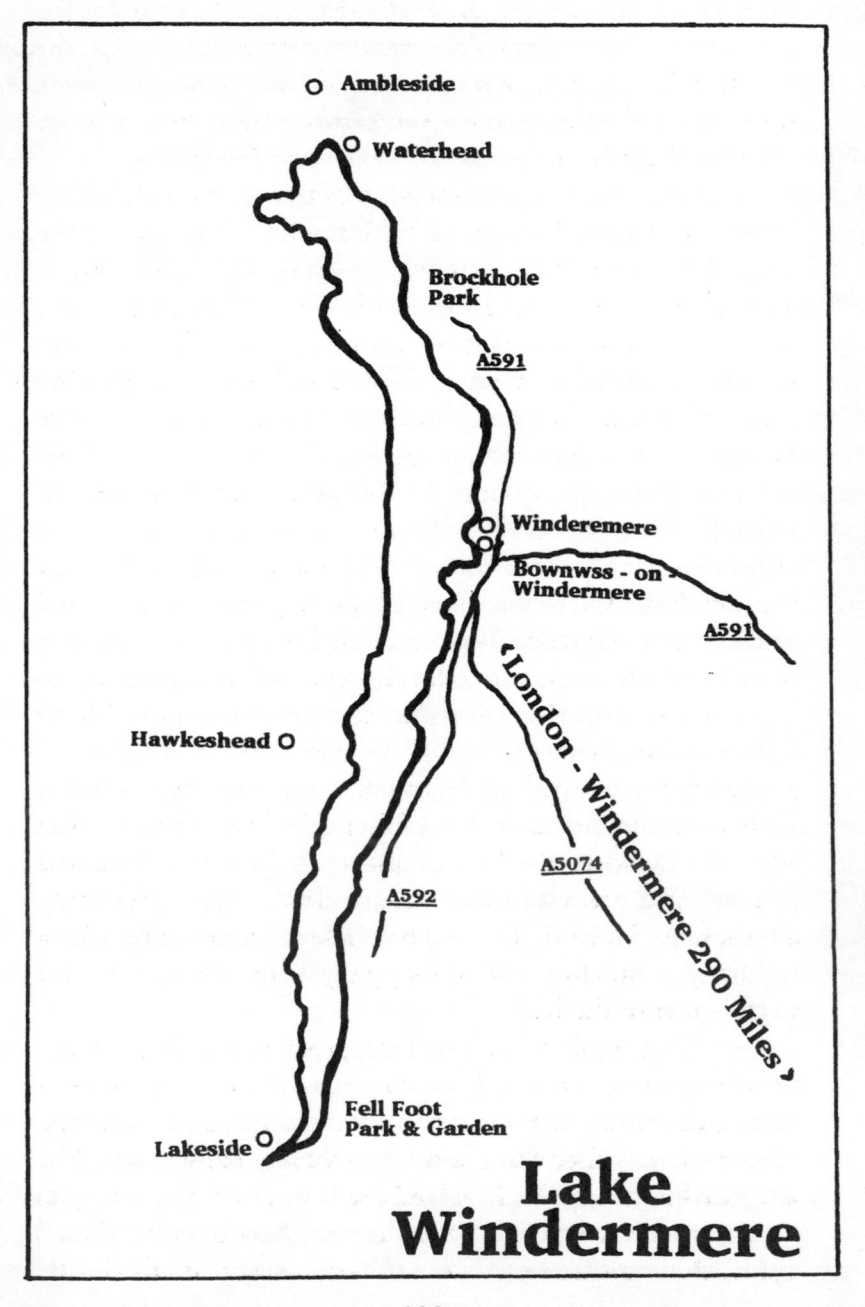

Ambleside

Waterhead

Brockhole
Park

A591

Windermere

Bownwss - on -
Windermere

A591

Hawkeshead

‹London - Windermere 290 Miles ›

A5074

A592

Fell Foot
Park & Garden

Lakeside

Lake
Windermere

referring to Grasmere, where he lived in Dove Cottage for the first years of the nineteenth century. And it is surely the countryside that inspired the children's stories of Beatrix Potter, who lived and wrote in the seventeenth-century stone cottage called Hill Top, near the hamlet of Sawrey, Ambleside.

This is an inspiring area to visit, dotted with quaint valley villages and outside cafes along lakeshore walks. We have been there a number of times, and felt that unless one is staying in a lovely and expensive hotel or guest house away from the crowded streets, one or two days are sufficient. Then we took command of the new 31-foot, dual helm motor cruiser *Miss Conistow* at the marina at Bowness and saw Windermere from an entirely different perspective.

The secret to staying in this most beautiful part of England is to be able to leave the crowded towns and lakeshore, yet to have access to its natural qualities. Still, at the same time the towns remain appealing and fun. Pubs and restaurants are bustling, shops are filled not only with people, but with goods ranging from local glassware, art and pottery to Scottish woolens, Kendall Mint Cakes and Cornish Clotted Cream Fudge. The crowds are actually very good-natured, polite and possessed with English reserve and courtesy. Perhaps it's the juxtaposition of shop-filled tourist towns, the lake, the steamers, the historic places and the wild hills and forests that create such an unusual and interesting atmosphere. Nevertheless, it's nice after a morning of hiking or biking or an afternoon of shopping, to be able to get away to the quiet of the lake.

A motor cruiser on the lake gives you access to the attractive but crowded towns, and also the natural surroundings. In fact, we felt a certain sense of smugness whenever we pulled our cruiser into a town marina or public jetty, tied up, stepped off, walked the streets, stopped for a pub lunch, sat on a waterside bench, and then stepped aboard again, alone within less than a minute, away from the bustle and commerce. Or we could moor along an isolated shore to walk through the woods, or rent a bicycle, then return to the privacy of our own place on the water. There was complete access to land and village activity, but no parking problems or congested streets and rarely difficulty in finding a place to tie up.

All told, Windermere is a relatively small lake when compared to the other natural cruising waters of Britain and Ireland such as the Norfolk Broads, the Thames, the Shannon and the chain of lakes of Scotland. The aim in renting a cruiser here is not so much long explorations of the lake itself, but the easy access it provides to the towns and countryside that surround it, while creating a home base for far less than the cost of the expensive hotels and inns of the area. And though many of the places to visit, from villages to parks, are close to the lakeshore, exploration farther afield can be accomplished by renting a car for a day, or taking the local bus. We especially recommend the nearby town of Grasmere, the drive north toward Pernrith along the especially beautiful valley lake called Ullswater, and along Coniston Water that parallels Lake Windemere, stopping at the villages of Coniston and Hawkshead, and nearby Beatrix Potter's Hill Top Farm.

Fauna & Flora

Like most rural spots long inhabited by humans and popular with tourists, the wildlife of Windermere is not very wild. The swans, geese, and ducks, congregate more at the town harbors where children feed them than in the more remote parts of the lake. In this respect, Windermere is not like the vast, thinly populated area of the South Norfolk Broads or the length of the River Shannon, remote from roads and other human presence. These lake verges are more like those of the Highland *lochs* of Scotland, rocky shores rather than reed marshes and fen that provide the habitat favored by many species. Nevertheless, boaters are rarely without the presence of waterfowl, tamer at the populated northern end and less so at the sparsely-settled southern end.

The hills are grass-covered, stony, and often bare in their higher slopes, while on the lower slopes they support deciduous and conifer forests easy to walk through. Were it not for the stonewalls, stone houses, mills, abbey ruins and ancient towns, the entire region would better resemble the foothills of the Sierras, the Cascades, or the Adirondacks. The mild climate and human occupancy assure prolific domestic plantings in the pretty towns of the area. An important garden, accessible to boaters at the southern tip of the lake, is the British National Trust's Fell Foot Park & Garden.

Highlights

Lake Windermere is a slender body, about eleven miles long and a mile wide, with a maximum depth of 210 feet. There is only one cruiser company on the lake, so all cruise itineraries must start at their boatyard at **Bowness-on-Windermere**. The town lies on the east shore roughly a third of the way down from the northern (top) end of the lake. Bowness joins with the town of **Windermere**, the two of them occupying a mile long stretch of the lake and well back into the hills. They are busy towns, not just as tourist havens, but as the commercial center for area residents. There are numerous hotels, inns, shops and the like, but little room for a supermarket along the winding streets, although there is a large one just above the main town center.

Lake Windermere is not so large that an itinerary needs to be worked out. The key to cruising there, and the pleasure of it, is to take a relaxed approach, going by whim or curiosity rather than by schedule. When you moor to walk in the woods or stop at a village for lunch, forget about a time schedule. Though, of course, on the afternoon of the first day of cruising you must settle on a direction out of the marina.

The southern end of the lake is by far the quieter, and is the best direction to start toward. The cruise downlake following the east shore is past a number of attractive old-fashioned buildings, spotted along the banks and rolling hilltops. Some are private homes, some are hotels, and some are clubs and outdoor activity centers. The jetties are often private, or for use by hotel guests, so watch for postings. Any jetty without a notice otherwise can be used. (Ask a staff member at the boatyard reception to mark your chart with company buoys and the best moorings.)

At the southern end, about an hour and a half cruising time from Bowness, many cruisers and sailing yachts are tied to buoys in a narrowing lake that becomes the end of navigation and the start of the **River Leven** that empties Lake Windermere into the sea at Morecamb Bay, fewer than three miles away. For the first night out we suggest tying to one of the cruiser company's buoys or, better, at the private **Lakeside Hotel** jetty. It's hard to miss the manicured grounds and tasteful eloquence of the hotel itself. There is an arrangement between the Lakeside Hotel and the boat company, so ignore the charge posted on the sign and simply walk to the hotel reception and tell them you are operating a Windermere Lake Holidays Afloat cruiser and that you'd like to use the pier. Dinner there on the first evening of cruising, or perhaps just tea, is a sure way of easing oneself from land-based civilization to life on a boat.

Across from the Lakeside is **Fell Foot Park**, an area owned by the British National Trust, a groomed, forested area surrounding a Victorian garden that has been restored to the beauty of its earlier days. There is a one-hour time limit at the jetty, especially during busy seasons and weekends, but this is a very worthwhile stop.

Adjacent to the Lakeside Hotel is the **Lakeside Station, Steamer Pier,** and **Aquarium**. From there antique passenger steamers ply the length of the lake between Lakeside and Ambleside, a small seasonal train operates, and the very good, if modest, aquarium is entertaining.

Uplake from Lakeside the shoreline is wooded, with coves, two kayaking centers, and a few moorings. From

Gubbins Point northward to **Rawlinson Nab** ("nab" in the local vernacular means a nose of land), the verge is a nesting area for waterfowl. Further north, across from the home-base boatyard, is the west shore terminal for the car ferry that connects Bowness with the road to Hawkshead village and Coniston Water. Ten minutes cruising from the ferry house, along the west shore of **Belle Island**, there are two idyllic company mooring buoys to tie to if you want peace and quiet.

The waters around **Bowness** are busy with private cruisers and sailing yachts and the marina is often full, but there are public moorings there, just fifteen minutes cruising time north of the home boatyard. They are not particularly inviting for overnight, but the location provides access to the town and the lakefront shops and pubs.

Uplake of the west shoreline is the quiet side, wooded and unpopulated, its northern end of close-in bays and coves filled with wildfowl and closed to power boats between March 1 and August 1. The east shore, however, is open all the way into Ambleside. From Bowness along the east shore are public jetties at **Rayrigg Meadow** (picnic grounds), the **National Trust Jetty** just beyond, and a mooring we especially like for overnight at **Brockhole Park**, some 40 minutes cruising from the Bowness home marina. From the jetty at Brockhole, it's a short walk through the woods to the **Lake District National Park Visitor's Centre**. NOTE: Tie only to the north side of the Brockhole jetty— DO NOT TIE to the red posts as the lake steamers come in often during the day.

Ambleside town center is back from the lake about a quarter mile, but there are piers at the shore for what is in effect its outskirt, called **Waterhead**. There is an **Information**

Mooring at Brockhole Park

Centre just across the street from the piers and the quay where a town map, brochure and other material and can be found. Of particular interest outside of the shops and restaurants are **The Armitt**, Ambleside's museum, St. Mary's Church, Adrian Sankey Glass Makers, and **Rydal Mount and Gardens** where Wordsworth lived from 1813 until his death in 1850. Bicycles can be rented at Bike Treks (Tel: 31505), there are several especially fine local walks that range from easy to breath-taking (ask at the Information Centre), and there are grocers for restocking the cruiser.

Best Times to Go

Given consideration of weather, crowded seasons and seasonal prices, early June and September are excellent times, followed by the month of May and even as early as the last week of April. This is a very small fleet, so plan well ahead, make an early decision, and *book at least six months in advance*.

Navigation Notes

There are no channel markers in the lake as in most of the larger waterways, only red DANGER markers. They are usually buoys, or sometimes posts along shallow water edges. The yellow buoys are fairway markers that are the guides and touchpoints for yacht racing. White buoys, sometimes with markings, are mooring buoys.

The small chart supplied with the boat is minimal, so purchase a copy of the large version that gives better detail on jetties and markers, and makes a nice souvenir. Also, ask a cruiser company staff member to mark the location of the company's private mooring buoys and reserved jetties on your chart. The lake can be crowded at times and many mooring buoys, docks, and jetties are private. However, *the public jetties marked with a time limit may be used for overnight mooring between the hours of about 6:00 p.m. and 8:00 a.m.*

Getting There

The Lake District has no specific central point, but for drivers guided by road signs, the principal cities in the Lake Windermere area are Kendall, ten miles east, just off the M6 motorway, and Windermere at the mid-point of the lakeshore. The distance from London is about 300 miles by highway.

For travelers without a vehicle, there is rail from London's Euston Station to Windermere via a stop at Oxenholme. From the station at Windermere the distance to central Bowness-on-Windermere is under two miles. The boatyard of the only cruiser rental company on the lake, Windermere Lake Holidays Afloat, is two miles from central Bowness, a taxi fare of about £3.50. Ask the driver to take you to Robson's Boatyard at the "Ferry Nab."

If driving, there is a short road about a half-mile south of the Bowness town center; watch for signs to "Hawkshead via Ferry." The narrow road appears to be one-way, lined with parked cars pointing to the lake, but pay no attention. They are waiting for the ferry, so just pass them by.

We recommend arrival in Britain a day or more before the cruising start day. This is normally a Saturday, but there is some flexibility in the early and late months of the year. Stay at least one overnight in a hotel or B&B near the boatyard in order to get over jet-lag and arrive refreshed on the morning of departure. This will give time for grocery shopping, loading luggage, and the hands-on training and introduction to the cruiser, the charts and the area. There are literally dozens of hotels and inns in the area, but two nice ones close to the marina are:

• The Burnside Hotel, Bowness-on-Windermere, Tel: 15394-42211, Fax: 15394-43842

• The Belsfield Hotel, Bowness-on-Windermere, Tel: 15394-42448, Fax: 15394-46397

For a very interesting start, arrive in the area early and stay at the Lakeside Hotel before cruising, then take the regular boat from the adjacent Steamer Pier to Bowness; the trip time is 40 minutes and departures are every hour and ten minutes. To get to the hotel, it is just off the A590 or, by rail on London's Euston Station-Glasgow line, get off at Oxenholm station and take a taxi to the hotel for about £12.

• Lakeside Hotel, Newby Bridge, Tel: 15395-31207, Fax: 15394-31699, E-mail: lshotel@aol.com

The Boat Rental Company
Windermere Lake Holidays Afloat
Robson's Boatyard
Ferry Nab
Bowness-on-Windermere, Cumbria LA23 3JH
Tel: 1539-443415 Fax: 1539-488721

There are a number of boat rental companies on the shores of the lake dealing with hourly and day rentals of small motorboats, rowboats and sailing yachts, but only Windermere Lake Holidays Afloat offers weekly rentals of substantial cruisers and sailing yachts. The small fleet of six cruisers and nine sailboats is based in a marina just north of the center of the east shore of Lake Windermere, a half mile south of Bowness town center.

This company has been in the boat business for over sixty years, the last twenty under the same ownership, and has certain rights deriving from its history that benefit its hire boat clients, such as a number of private mooring buoys and mooring rights at key jetties around the lake.

The reception area is above a company-owned store that sells everything from waterproof jackets and items of chandlery to postcards. Its primary clientele has long been domestic, but it is interested in reaching a more international group. We found, for example, that linens had to be rented in advance and that towels were not provided at all because local and most continental clients brought their own, something that overseas visitors would not do. Towels are now provided as part of the linens package, but *they must be booked at the time of the boat booking*.

The marina is small and a bit crowded, but easily accessible by car/taxi so that luggage and grocery transfer is simple. (Week-long parking is available to clients at no cost).

The choice of vessels is small, but the boats are well-designed and modern, with two new ones added recently. They are "sport" or "sedan" style, but in all of them the steering position is not exposed to the elements. There is only one boat (two singles and a convertible in the salon) that is adequate for two for a week, but for the full berth compliment of four persons it would be cramped. Consider it for two couples or small family only if you are looking for economy. Otherwise, even for a couple we suggest the new four-berth *Miss Coniston* or the older four-berth dual-helm *Commodore 31*. The largest, *Miss Eskdale*, sleeps four comfortably, six in a pinch, or a family of two adults and four children quite well. The prices are modest, and even at peak season the average rent for a cruiser is less than equivalent space in hotel rooms in the towns.

A good selection of sailing yachts is available, including two 35-foot yachts that comfortably sleep six. The largest require previous sailing experience, but adequate training is

Steamer on Lake Windermere

available for people with no experience. This is a good opportunity for anyone who has ever wanted to sail.

The instruction for cruisers, as well as for yachts, is well done. Half an hour at the jetty and a turn on the lake near the marina is plenty to make even novices feel adequate for skippering a cruiser. Sailing instruction takes longer and should be arranged at the time of booking.

Overall, this is an easy company to deal with and to learn from if instruction is needed. Ask for a Lakeside Hotel Pass (discounts on food and use of the showers) and pass to the private Windermere Marina Village Spinnaker Club. If you prefer the combination of a self-catering lakeside apartment and a rented dayboat to explore the lake, ask about the company's accommo-dation overlooking the marina. They were just finishing restoration of a handsome old stone house, so two large apartments are new and should be quite special. Also, shorter rental periods than a week are often available in periods off the peak season.

To book, contact the company directly or one of the agents: Blakes Boating Holidays (UK Tel: 1603-782911, 784141; Fax: 1603-782871; E-mail: boats@blakes.co.uk; Website: www.blakes.co.uk or one of the US agents: Great Trips Unlimited (Tel: 888-329-9720; E-mail: admin@gtunlimited.com; Website: www.gtunlimited.com) or Blakes Vacation (Tel: 800-628-8188; E-mail: blakes1076@aol.com; Website: www.blakesvacations.com). Alternatively, select one of the cruisers mentioned above in confidence and phone the company or an agent and ask about availability, then pay the required deposit by credit card.

CHAPTER 5

England: Other Natural Waterways

There are three other waterways in Britain on which there are rental cruisers available: The Great Ouse & Cam, The Yorkshire Ouse, and the Severn & Avon. Each is important in its own way; each is in a different but interesting region. They are, however, relatively minor when contrasted to the Norfolk Broads, the Thames, or Scotland's Highland lakes. Of the three, the waterways of Cambridgeshire and Yorkshire in the east of England are the most accessible to overseas travelers, with or without a rental car.

At present there are only three cruiser hire companies involved, one in each of the river systems. But the rivers flow through countrysides and numerous towns very much worth visiting, and although there are narrowboats on some, the scarcity of other rental cruisers on these waters adds a certain appeal. To give an idea, there are a total of only about thirty rental cruisers on the three waterways that combined extend for well over 250 miles. That's fewer than the number in one modest fleet at a boatyard in the Norfolk Broads.

One reason, we suspect, the Great Ouse and Cam that flow through Cambridgeshire are less popular with cabin cruiser boaters is that there are locks to contend with, whereas the Broads are lock-free and those of the Thames are handled by lockkeepers. On the Great Ouse, for example, there are seventeen locks, all of them single-gate vertical lift (like a guillotine) that require many turns of the lifting winch both up, then down, to meet the requirement of leaving the gate lowered. They are, however, no more complex than those along the popular canals of Britain, and are most certainly not so demanding that these fine waterways should be overlooked.

Another reason may be the nature of these smaller eastern rivers themselves: they are not broad like most of the Thames, far less grand than the Shannon, and they lie in countryside far less dramatic than the lakes of Scotland's Great Glen. Instead, they can best be characterized as tranquil and slow-flowing, not very wide, often seeming more like a winding canal than a proper river. These features, however, are their assets, drawing boaters who prefer uncrowded, often isolated, stretches whose banks are enhanced often by pretty towns and villages, as well as by the natural areas through which they flow.

With the caveat that the authors are less acquainted with them than with the major systems that comprise the main body of this guide, they are nevertheless touched on here, called to the attention of readers who might prefer the independence and the adventure of travel on waterways less described.

Cambridgeshire's Great Ouse & The Cam

Overview

Five rivers comprise the waterway navigable by motor cruisers in this lovely part of England, two of which are the famous Cam and the Great Ouse (not to be confused with the Ouse in Yorkshire, described in the next section). Then there are three smaller rivers that feed the main stem: the Lark, the Little Ouse, and the River Wissey. Overall they open over 140 miles of meandering river to boaters, some passing through what are among the most important and picturesque cities, towns, and villages of England.

Called the Fenland, or the Fens, centered some sixty miles northeast of London, the westward area toward the source of the Cam in Northamptonshire is a countryside of rolling hills, while toward the east some of the area is treeless wetland and meadowland for grazing. Toward the east, the verges along open water are often marshes where reeds and sedges dominate. These are hard areas to explore on foot, often boggy, often hardly more than a thin layer of roots and plants overlaying liquid, yet in addition to the birdlife they support, they are complex ecosystems in which grow a multitude of plants. Although walking paths criss-cross the eastern fens, they are easily explored by boat along the waterways. They can be delicate areas and must be gently dealt with. Reedy areas of the fens are the nesting place for black headed gulls who build on the surface, and reed and sedge warblers whose nests surround the stalks.

The carr that is the transition zone between fen and dryland forest, is also hard to walk through and can be damaged in the process, but from the waterway its character and wildlife can be seen, experienced and photographed.

Thus, the countryside slopes gently from the low hills of western Cambridgeshire to a generally flat east, a mix of meadow, marsh and drained waterside land with some larger growth and trees. The unpopulated stretches are rich with birdlife, including woodcocks, woodpeckers, redpolls, siskin and blackcaps—in addition to the waterfowl and reed-dwellers. Coarse fishing for bream, pike, rudd, and the like attracts many boat and bank anglers.

Highlights

For travelers from overseas, especially persons seeking quintessential old England, it is the towns along the rivers that are the main attraction of this area—though even better is the combination of the towns, rivers, and rural countryside. It is because of the rivers that the towns were founded in the first place, communities that grew along the watery commercial corridors of medieval times and before. The towns themselves, especially the smaller ones, retain an atmosphere born of their ancient association with the rivers, and even larger ones like **Bedford** and **Cambridge** still offer an invitation to boaters. Who has not seen images of students and lovers idly punting on the **Cam** under the **Bridge of Sighs**? This is not to say that cruising along the tranquil rivers themselves is not appealing, only that having destinations such as **St. Ives** and **St. Neots** adds interest.

The boatyard at **Ely** lies near the midpoint of the river system, so the first decision is which way to go, upstream or down. Discuss this on arrival, as there may be local or seasonal reasons to choose one direction over the other, but we suggest starting up the **Ouse** along the Old West River toward **St. Ives** and **Huntingdon.** There are four locks between Ely and Huntingdon. You will be taught how to operate these before departing the boatyard, and in the process will learn whether or not you want to proceed past Huntingdon to Bedford, a stretch on which there are fourteen more locks. The time for the full Ely-Bedford round-trip is about a week, but by making a few early starts it's possible to cruise the full distance *plus* a trip up the Cam to Cambridge and return, either before or after cruising the Great Ouse.

Bedford, at the western end of navigation of the Great Ouse, is a city of about 80,000 and offers to boaters the lovely Priory Marina Park. The Bunyan Trail, named after the John Bunyan of *Pilgrim's Progress* fame, offers glimpses into his life and times at the Bunyan Library and museum. Downriver from Bedford there are moorings at the interesting village stops of **Willington, Roxton,** and then **St. Neots** to visit the **St. Mary the Virgin Church**. These, and towns like **Great Paxton** and **Huntingdon** (birthplace of Oliver Cromwell and site of the Cromwell museum), should be visited in leisure. It is these town stops that make cruising the rivers of Cambridgeshire so rewarding.

On returning down the Great Ouse, if you have made the time cruise up the Cam into **Cambridge** (two locks between the confluence of the Cam and Ouse and the city). The last time we drove through Cambridge town (in late 1998) we were somewhat overwhelmed by the changes during the past decade, mostly caused by traffic and the consequent difficulty in finding a place to park anywhere near the university and center of the city. By boat, simply wander along the River Cam and moor (although in July and August even finding a mooring spot can be difficult). It is, nevertheless, an excellent way of accessing Cambridge. From April 1 to October 1 the end of navigation is at **Jesus Lock** in Cambridge, which means a long walk, taxi or public transportation to the colleges and central city. Or, better, rent a punt and give punting on the Cam a try, or hire a student-operated punt. Between October 1 and April 1 the river is open to cruising as far as the "backs," meaning the beautiful grassy strip along several of the colleges. Visit at least **Magdalene College** (pronounced *maudlin*), **Trinity College,** and **Christ's College**. Even during the period that the Cam is open past the backs, the end of cruiser navigation is at Mill Lane. Further travel through the countryside upriver to **Grantchester** is by hired punt.

For travelers who are planning just one week, the reason for itineraries focusing on a trip up and down the Great Ouse and up and down the Cam, is that the towns and countryside south of Ely along both of these rivers are more interesting than downriver of Ely. They will absorb the major part of your time. It doesn't matter the order of the river choice, Cam first or the Great Ouse first, and the decision can be reached after arrival by discussing the options with the boatyard staff. In either case, this will leave the stretch of the Great Ouse below Ely, and the cruises up the three branches (**Lark, Little Ouse**, and **Wissey**) to the amount of time you have left, if any. In other words, it's not feasible to cover the entire 140 miles (225 km) of the five rivers in a week, so it's better to run out of time having not visited Stoke Ferry at the far end of the River Wissey than having not visited Cambridge near the head of the Cam or Bedford near the head of the Great Ouse.

Returning down the Cam (or Great Ouse), the river passes your starting point, **Ely**. If you did not visit this delightful cathedral town before cruising, plan to spend time there afterward, either on the last day of cruising or from a land-based accommodation. There are good moorings in the lee of the fourteenth-century cathedral and near the **Maltings**, a former brewery converted into a concert stage.

Downriver of Ely, before the end of navigation at Denver Sluice some seventeen miles away, the rivers Lark (thirteen navigable miles), Little Ouse (thirteen miles) and the Wissey (ten miles) enter the Great Ouse from the east. Although they go through small towns, the countryside is rural, quite flat, and rather isolated.

We suggest an early arrival in Ely in order to start your cruising adventure refreshed. It is also a splendid and important town to visit. Two good choices for accommodations are:

• Lamb Hotel, 2 Lynn Rd., Ely, Cambridgeshire Tel: 1353-663574

• Nyton Hotel, 7 Barton Road, Ely, Cambridgeshire Tel: 1353-662459, Fax: 1353-666217

For others in the area, try:
http://www.smoothhound.co.uk/ely.html

Best Times to Go
Definitely from mid-April to mid-June and again in September into early October. Since there are not many hire cruisers available in the area, it's important to *book in advance three to four months* for the peak summer months, two months for the shoulder seasons and none at all for other times (except Easter holidays).

The Rental Boat Company
Bridge Boatyard
Bridge Rd, Ely, Cambridgeshire, CB7 4DY
Tel: 1353-663726 Fax: 1353-668766
Website: www.hoseasons.co.uk

This small boat company, the last on the Cam and Cambridgeshire Ouse, has been in business for nearly thirty years and offers a nice selection from a fleet of nineteen cruisers. Of these, some are sliding-top Broads-style with forward or center steering and some are traditional aft-steering, including the ultra-modern *Sunray*, an excellent cruiser for two. For four persons, the *Sunquest* is the best choice.

There are several start days offered by the company, Monday, Friday or Saturday, which helps travelers flying the Atlantic.

The marina, near the center of the wonderful cathedral city of Ely, is easy to get to, as is Ely itself. There are at least eight trains daily out of London's Liverpool station, and the Bridge Boatyard is only a few hundred yards from the Ely railway station. If loaded with luggage, take a taxi or walk over to the boatyard and ask for a ride.

Book direct or through Hoseasons; direct booking will enable you to ask questions of people who know the territory. The price is the same, except for the small service fee for booking through the US agent (Tel: 800-662-2628).

Yorkshire's River Ouse & Ripon Canal

Overview & Highlights
We sat in the lounge of a cruiser moored at the boatyard of York Marine at Bishopthorpe on the **Yorkshire Ouse** and talked with Dave Smith, riverman and company operator, about boats, moorings, pubs, and itineraries. Earlier that week

we'd chatted with boaters tied up along the Ouse north of the city of **York**, and in the **Ripon Canal** off the Ouse not far from where we were staying, and on the moorings at the heart of the York, a stone's throw from the great York Minster. In fact, the most appealing feature of cruising this gentle river is the varied environments through which it passes, from the bustling center of York to the peaceful Yorkshire countryside both to the north and the south of the boatyard.

About an hour of pleasant cruising downstream of the marina at **Bishopthorpe**, the Ouse becomes tidal and navigation ends at the moorings and village of **Naburn**.

In the other direction, upstream an hour or so is York itself, with much activity along the riverbanks, from pubs to inns, and moorings that enable access to the magnificent sites and sights of that great city. Beyond York the river winds its way in a northwesterly direction through relatively flat countryside past villages like **Benningbrough**, **Newton-on-Ouse**, and **Linton-on-Ouse**.

About thirty river miles above York the first of a series of locks is encountered, of which there are four on the Ouse and two more on the Ripon Canal for anyone wanting to go on into that lovely historic cathedral town. The locks are manually operated, requiring some effort (but not too much), but as there are thirty-seven miles of open river between the nearest northern lock and Naburn village to the south of the boatyard, it's easy to fill and enjoy a week without going into the lock system at all. Our advice to anyone not wanting to put in this small effort is simply to stay downriver of the locks—there is plenty to see and do. Nevertheless, the task of going through the locks and into the canal is rewarded by the attractive and busy town, and especially a visit to **Ripon Cathedral**, one of the most beautiful and interesting in England. It is the town and church of Charles Lutwidge Dodgson who, as **Lewis Carroll**, was the author whose most notable books include *The Hunting of the Snark, Through the*

Looking Glass, Alice in Wonderland, and *Symbolic Logic.* It is believed that some of the intricately carved bench ends and other wood carvings in the cathedral, where his father, the archdeacon of Richmond, was a canon, were the inspiration for many of the ideas and strange creatures that inhabit Carroll's stories. Look especially for the griffin and rabbits misericord on the mayor's seat, the rabbit going into its hole on a bench end. A splendid day can be spent in **Ripon**, much of it at the busy cathedral, where a great slice of English history comes alive.

In order to start cruising refreshed after a transatlantic flight, an early arrival in York makes sense. Good hotels there include the Best Westward Dean Court Hotel, wonderfully located in Duncombe Place near York Minster (Tel: 1904-625082; Fax: 1904-620305, or in the US 800-528-1234); or the 3-star Mount Royale Hotel, 119 The Mount (Tel: 1904-628856; Fax: 1904-611171). For other York hotels, try www.britain.co.uk/pages/yorkhotelsall.htm.

Itineraries
The York Marine boatyard is near the lower end of the Ouse, so it is immaterial whether you head off downstream, turn and pass by the boatyard en route to York and Ripon, then retrace back to the boatyard, or vice versa. However, if you are departing in mid-afternoon, we suggest cruising downstream for a stop at the **Ship Inn Pub** for supper, and an overnight mooring there at **Naburn**.

Best Times to Go
Definitely from mid-April to mid-June and again in September into early October. Since there are not many hire cruisers available in the area, it's important to *book in advance three to four months* for the peak summer months, two months for the shoulder seasons and none at all for other times (except Easter holidays).

The Boat Rental Company

York Marine Services Ltd.
Ferry Lane
Bishopthorpe, York YO2 1B
Tel: 1904-704442 /705815 Fax: 1904-705824
E-mail: bookings@holidayuk.co.uk
Website: www.holidayuk.co.uk/afloat/yorkmarine/index.htm
This is the only hire boat company on the Yorkshire Ouse. In addition to renting motor cruisers, York Marine offers day hire of small outboard boats, a restaurant on site, cruises, and sightseeing on the Ouse into the heart of the city of York.

This is a small rental boat operation with nine cruisers, most of which are broad-beam, single-front helm boats with a sliding canopy over the living/dining area. Only the two-berth *Sunrise* and the two-plus-two berth *Sunburst* are of conventional design: small sedan-type cruisers with a folding canopy. They should be avoided unless there is a guarantee of sunny weather. The others are designed all on one level with a long hallway running between the aft and the lounge area with cabins along the hall. These Broads-type cruisers are very convenient and offer a maximum use of space. What they lack in height they make up for in length (37 feet is typical for a six-berth boat). Most of the fleet has been purchased used, mostly from Norfolk Broads operators, then re-fitted and restored. They are not the latest models, but they are inexpensive to rent, clean, comfortable, and easy to manage. For two, we favor the *Sundancer*, but either the *Sunbeam* or *Sunchaser* would do.

In addition to a well-illustrated captain's manual, a key is given to boaters who may want to use the facilities provided by British Waterways, including showers at certain moorings. Some boaters prefer these over the showers on board. These moorings with facilities are at Naburn, Boroughbridge, and the Ripon Canal.

The reason for booking with this company is not the boats or the marina, but the River Ouse and the proximity of the boatyard to the center of the city of York and, upriver of York, the tranquility of the river and its course through the Yorkshire countryside. A journey on the Ripon Canal into the town of Ripon is a plus for anyone willing to cruise through the two simple locks.

There are many train departures daily between London's Kings Cross Station (and other cities) and the City of York. Once in York, take a taxi for a fare of about £5. If driving, take Bishopthorpe Road from central York into the village of Bishopthorpe. Pass the Bishopthorpe Palace (sharp bend in the road), take the first left (Acaster St.), go fifty yards and turn left on Ferry Lane. The reception office and boatyard are at the end of the lane.

Unlike most boat companies, the start day can be any day set at time of booking. Arrive early if you need to rest after a flight, but leave the exploration of York to a time of mooring in the city center. For catalog & booking, contact the boatyard directly or Blakes.

The Avon and The Severn

Overview & Highlights

This is a region of rolling hills, a mostly rural area spotted with old and pretty towns, many of them situated on the rivers **Avon** and **Severn**. Often referred to as the heart of England, the counties of **Gloucestershire**, **Hereford**, **Worcester**, **Warwick**, and **Oxford** are where towns with names familiar to many foreigners lie: **Tewkesbury**, **Gloucester**, **Evesham**, **Stow-on-the-Wold**, **Broadway**, and **Stratford-upon-Avon** among them. Tour buses travel the narrow "B" roads and tourists wander the streets of these popular spots.

A look at the map of England shows the breadth of the Severn; its miles-wide estuary separates England from Wales, then diminishes rapidly upriver from the city of **Gloucester**. The Severn is closed to hire-boat navigation at Gloucester, where a series of locks separates the river from its tidal estuary.

153

It can nevertheless be a somewhat unruly river—not a rampaging one, but it certainly has periods when it becomes very wide in flood. Consequently, the containment banks mean that when the Severn is at its normal height, it is impossible to see the countryside from the boat. The upshot: the Severn is unpredictable and not among the better cruising rivers of Britain.

The Avon, on the other hand, is tame and peaceful, flowing between low banks that make countryside sightseeing just fine. There is birdlife and other wildlife, but the interesting character of the waterway is the towns and villages that lie along it. Moorings are plentiful, and it's easy to tie up and explore the towns.

Itineraries

For a week of cruising, cruiser company owner John Bullock's recommendation is to travel down the Severn from the boatyard to its confluence with the Avon at Tewkesbury, then turn into the Avon via a lock at the Gateway to the Avon, then up to Stratford-upon-Avon, then return. This will take the week at a leisurely pace, allowing time to stop along the way to visit waterside towns, and to enjoy an occasional lunch, afternoon break or dinner at some of the many inns and pubs that are spaced along the riverside. At a less leisurely pace, it's possible to again join the Severn at Tewkesbury and turn south for a day of exploration, especially down to Gloucester to visit the bustling Gloucester Docks, where tall ships once moored, and now the site of a museum, pubs, and shops. As mentioned, the Avon is also the more dependable of the two in terms of constant water height—but that means more locks. Except for the manned locks at Tewkesbury and Evesham, these are manually operated by the boat crew, but they are small, easy to operate (you'll be taught how) and two people can easily handle them.

Best Times to Go

As with the other rivers in this chapter, the best times to go are from mid-April to mid-June and again in September into early October. With only two boats available, the advance booking time needed is hard to predict. Definitely plan six months ahead for July and August, and four months for other times (except after mid-October and before April 1).

The Boat Rental Company

Gulliver's Cruisers, Ltd.
Upton-on-Severn
Tel: 1684-593400 Fax: 1684-565964

There is only one cruiser rental company operating on the entire Severn-Avon rivers system, and it is a small one. In Upton-on-Severn, north of the nearby town of Tewkesbury, we found Gulliver's Cruisers. There is no office or reception room, e-mail or website; the operation basically consists of the affable John Bullock working out of his home, with his two cruisers lost among literally dozens of private boats in the Upton-on-Severn Marina. Neither member of the small fleet was available for our use at the time, so we had to explore the countryside by car, a less rewarding experience, we are sure. Nevertheless, Mr. Bullock knows the rivers and was most helpful by offering information and advice. Talking and planning with him would be the best approach for anyone wanting to cruise in the area.

The number of boats located at the large marina where Gulliver's small fleet is based indicated clearly the popularity of these rivers for pleasure cruising.

The choice of vessels is easy. There is a conventional cabin cruiser that sleeps four and a long, broad-beam Broads cruiser that we looked at as it was preparing for departure. It sleeps four adults and a child, and we recommend it even for two, as it provides a remarkable amount of space (and even boasts a small bathtub in one of the bathrooms). But the former would do, as well.

For travelers without a rental car, there is frequent rail service from London's Paddington Station to Birmingham New Street, then a change to the line to Hereford via Great Malvern. From Great Malvern it is a twelve-mile taxi ride to the boatyard.

If possible, it's good to arrive the day before the cruising start day, so consider asking the Bullocks to book a room at the Red Lion Hotel in Upton-on-Severn.

There is no agent, so booking is made directly by telephone or fax (no e-mail yet). The Bullocks will answer all your questions. In spite of its size, the tiny company is nevertheless worth note here, and we are confidant that someone will make contact from this side of the Atlantic and occupy one of the only two hire cruisers presently on the Avon-Severn waterway.

CHAPTER 6

Scotland: The Highland Lakes & the Great Glen

Glen More and Glen Albyn are among the various names given to the very long geological fault, the Great Rift, whose surface features run for nearly sixty miles in a Northeast-Southwest direction between the city of Inverness at the northerly end and Ft. William at the southern. Out of sight it sinks beneath the surface of the sea at both ends, the displacement being obvious only to scientists who know that it extends for many miles out the Moray Firth and into the North Sea. At the other end it forms Loch Linnhe and the Firth of Lorne before the ocean bed goes deep beneath the Atlantic.

On a land scoured by glaciers many millennia ago, the most obvious signs of the Great Rift are the fresh water lakes and the rivers that it cradles: Loch Dochfour, Loch Ness, and the River Ness at the northeast, Loch Oich and the River Oich next, and Loch Lochy and the River Lochy that fills the staircase of locks and spills into the sea at Ft. William.

These great lakes and the connecting waterways, some of them natural, some hand made, form what is also called the **Caledonian Canal.** Together they are a slender body of water that lies along the rift from which a land of wild yet tranquil beauty rises, and along which are a few small towns, a few castles, woodlands, picnic sites, footpaths, the occasional waterside restaurant, and most important to boaters, moorings.

Inverness Tourist Information Centre:
Bridge Street
Tel: 1463-234353; Fax: 1463-710609 (open all year)

Scottish Tourist Board:
www.holiday.scotland.net/welcome

Highland Scottish Tourist Board:
www.host.co.uk/welcome
Also, a very good private website has been created by
Joanne MacKenzie-Winters:
www.scotland-info.co.uk/inverness

International Telephone Code:
011-44-
City Codes:
Inverness 1463, Edinburgh 131

The name Caledonian Canal is in a way an unfortunate choice because it conjures an image of a narrow channel filled with narrow boats and old locks. It is anything but that. Yet to deny its latter day origins is to deny a feat of great design and construction. The lakes of the Great Glen were once separate, connected and fed only by uncontrolled rivers along which passage was difficult at best. Yet as early as the seventeenth century there were dreams of creating a navigable waterway between the two seas, a canal through which full-rigged sailing ships could pass. It was two centuries before the immense task was undertaken, and eighteen years passed from the time the work began until it was completed. Thomas Telford, a remarkable man responsible for many feats of construction and canal building in Britain, underestimated the extent and ultimate cost of the project of twenty miles of waterway, at £912,000—about $4.5 million in 1804—but nevertheless carried to completion what was doomed to soon become a monument to grand dream and effort, but little more.

Beginning in 1822 a few passenger ships from Liverpool and Glasgow sailed the new link to Inverness, but by 1847 the waterway ceased to be maintained, and Loch Ness remained the only lake on which there was commercial traffic. The regularly scheduled passenger ships between Inverness and Ft. Augustus ended in 1930. It is now a vast waterway that has reverted to its former quiet nature save for a very few small commercial freight haulers, slow-going cabin cruisers, sailing yachts, and a wide-beam Dutch barge called the *Spirit of Loch Ness*. Now converted into a luxury hotel vessel it offers three- to six-night cruises for up to twelve passengers. The affable Robin Black is a good skipper, a wonderful host and the food on board is excellent! (Tel/Fax: 1463-711913)

Fauna & Flora

The rugged, glacier-scoured nature of the Great Glen makes spotting wildlife more difficult than on the other waterways of Britain and Ireland that are more vast and feature areas of marshes, carr and waterside forests. Here the land is forested in coniferous and deciduous trees which, coupled with a latitude roughly that of northern Newfoundland and Juneau, Alaska, gives an awareness of being quite far north, especially during the long days of summer. The steep slopes that meet the water's edge give little chance for the growth of cattails, reeds and other marshy growth. Nevertheless, grebes and Canada geese are companions to boaters, along with herons and smaller birds such as gray wagtails, white-chested dippers, common gulls and black-headed gulls. Sedge warblers and reed bunting can be spotted where the lakeshores flatten, while the kingfisher are more rare at this northern limit of their habitat. Loch Dochfour, just south of Inverness town, and the first of the lochs that cruisers enter from the north, is home to numerous ducks, including the diving golden-eye.

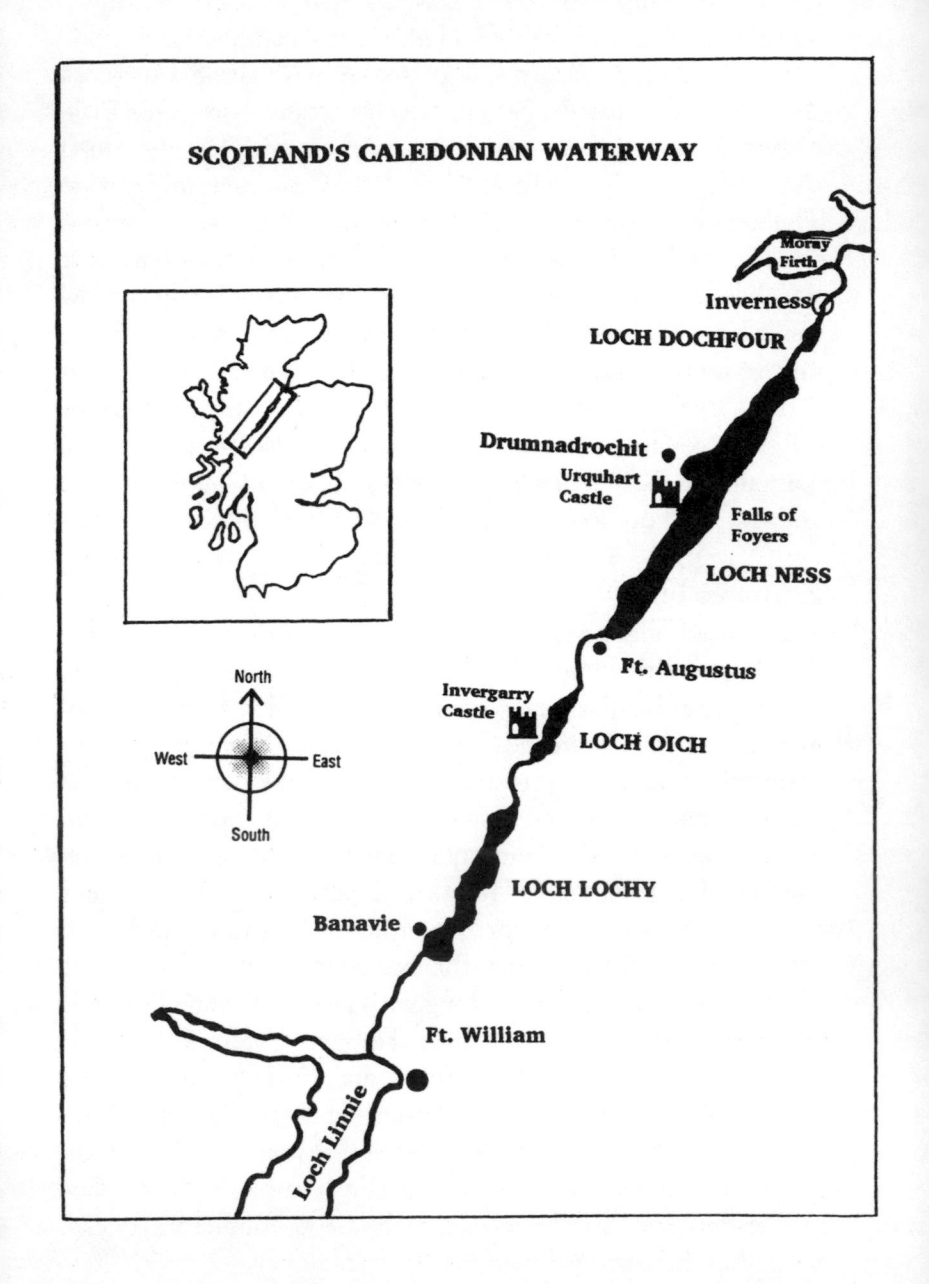

Scotland: The Highland Lakes & the Great Glen

Although relatively low in nutrients, the lakes are rich enough to support a modest population of resident fish and, therefore, fish-eating birds such as cormorants, red-breasted mergansers and goosanders. The most common fish in Loch Ness are pike, eel, lamprey, salmon, trout, stickleback, and arctic char, the latter of which is quite rare in the rest of Britain, requiring the cold, deep waters of Loch Ness. Salmon and sea trout run up the rivers at both ends of the glen and sport fishing is popular during season, as is trout fishing in the smaller lakes. Though judging from the relative scarcity of poles sticking out from passing cruisers, fishing in the large highland lakes is not the main aim of most boaters who come long distances to cruise and take in the ambience of the woods, castles, and towns.

Although the upper slopes of the hard rock mountains that lie parallel to the lochs are generally devoid of trees, the shores have abundant and various growth. Their nature depends on soil conditions, with Scots pine favoring acidic soils. Many of the forested pockets exhibit a rich mix of tree varieties, both conifer and broad-leaved species such as hazel, oak, ash and, of course, the ubiquitous birch of northern temperate zones. The shorelines are most typically not boggy or reedy, but where they are, and on the floors of the more ancient forests at Inverfarigaig (Loch Ness) and at Ach an Todhair near the Ft. William end, a remarkable mixture of ground cover can be found. At Inverfarigaig, look for blaeberry, dog's mercury, bugle, woodsage, bracken, and wild strawberries. In the few spots where marshes can be seen along with grassy meadowlands, look for orchids, of which at least nine species have been identified. Forests like Inverfarigaig and Ach an Todhair are accessible to walkers from boat moorings and clearly marked on the navigation charts.

For further reading, a concise overview is *The Great Glen: Wildlife & Landscape* published by the Nature Conservancy Council for Scotland, Fraser Darling House, 9 Culduthel Rd., Inverness IV2 4AG, United Kingdom. Write for a copy ahead of time, or buy at the tourist offices or boatyards in Invernesshire.

Highlights

Inverness is the home of the largest and oldest boat rental company in Scotland, and as the Scottish city most easily reached by overseas visitors traveling by air, rail, or bus from Heathrow or Gatwick, it is the ideal point from which to begin a water exploration of the Scottish waterway. (If driving, **Laggan**, the site of the other Scottish boatyard, is slightly closer.)

Inverness is a beautiful small city divided by the River Ness and the Caledonian Canal that runs parallel to the river. It is well worth some time and attention, either before or after the boat journey. We suggest arrival there at least a day prior to your cruiser start date, to rest if you've just arrived from overseas, and to look around. Though its residential sprawl is not too attractive, it is still an interesting old town, with plenty of shops, good restaurants, and pubs in the heart of the city. It's a short taxi run from the town center to the marina.

Some of the most important sites around the city include the ever-present **Inverness Castle**, built in 1835, that stands above the city and the river. At present it houses the Sheriffs Court and is open to the public daily from 10:30 AM to 5:30 PM. Don't miss walking the town center streets with their many sixteenth- and seventeenth-century buildings; a visit to **Saint Andrew's Cathedral** is also worthwhile. Stop by the Inverness Tourist Information Centre on Bridge Street for more information (Tel: 1463-234353).

The departure south from the **Caley Cruisers Marina** is along a wide, winding canal through one swing-bridge and one lock. Both are operated by keepers well accustomed to novice boaters. This seven-mile stretch provides an easy way to become accustomed to the cruiser—it is easy navigation and the water is deep almost to the shore. Just past the **Dochgarroch Lock** the Caledonian Canal joins the **River Ness**, where the combined waterway quickly broadens into small **Loch Dochfour**. For an introduction to the flora of the area, before going into **Loch Ness** visit the so-called "shingle" beach at **Aldourie**, on the east bank of the river where sea campion, herb-Robert and enchanter's nightshade grow. Fifteen minutes later you enter the twenty-three-mile-long Loch Ness, known throughout the world in part for its beauty, but mostly for its aquatic dragon of old, the **Loch Ness Monster.** We did not spot the monster, nor did we look very hard, but a day after we had cruised from the south end of the lake we chatted with a couple from Yorkshire who were fishing off a jetty in **Loch Oich**. They said that the previous June they had been trying to find the deepest spot in the loch with their depthfinder/fish locator, when at 666 feet depth the finder showed a vast, undulating reflection, either a dense school of fish or, as she believes, the monster itself. Who knows? But an industry has been built around belief in the creature. Loch Ness itself contains a greater volume of water than all the other lakes and rivers of England and Wales combined. It is not the longest, widest or deepest (average depth 430 feet), but the product of its dimensions makes it by far the greatest.

Boaters who want to ease into loch cruising by stopping to recover from jet-lag and spend the first night not far from the start can do so by mooring in **Brackla Harbor,** where the **Clansman Hotel** and its fine pub stand looking across the lake. Beyond that, the second convenient mooring, half an hour beyond, is **Urquhart Bay** where there is a £7 fee for overnight mooring. This is the only fee spot on the waterway, and the money goes to support a good community cause; the mooring is convenient and pretty, too. It is 1½ miles from the mooring to the village of **Drumnadrochit**.

Across Urquhart Bay, standing on a high promontory and the site of a more ancient fort, is **Urquhart Castle**, a handsome sixteenth-century ruin half surrounded by clipped lawn, tall forest, and Loch Ness. There is an admission charge of about £3, but it makes for a delightful stop and exploration.

A kilted piper is sometimes there, especially when a wedding is being held at this popular place. We had to tie our cruiser to the wedding boat, a Caley Cruiser similar to ours, and from a little distance took in the entire grand affair, culminating when the wedding party boarded their cruiser and champagne flowed. We had to cross their boat to get to ours and couldn't help becoming involved when on the top deck they handed us full stems of the sparkling wine. It was the first time we'd seen a kilted skipper and a crew of kilted men and gowned ladies on a cruiser.

The Urquhart jetty is small, reserved on one side for Caley hire cruisers. If full, tie to another boat. If you must tie to the other side of the jetty, watch for the small passenger boats to arrive. It is a stop on their cruise route and the place is reserved.

Across the lake from Urquhart Castle at **Inverfarigiag** pier is an interesting exhibit of the **Forestry Commission** and marked paths through a small but wonderful forest. Tying there should be tried only when the weather is fair and the winds low, and it should not be used for overnight mooring.

Just fifteen cruising minutes south of the Inverfarigiag forest center there is another mooring, blighted somewhat by a hydroelectric station, but interesting nonetheless for its mile-long forest walk up to the cascades of **Foyer Falls**.

Ft. Augustus, at the southwestern end of Loch Ness, about three hours from Urquhart Castle, is a perfect spot to moor overnight. The loch narrows very little, the entry to the canal is straight and easy, and the setting of the quay below the walls and towers of **St. Benedict's Abbey** brings one into a different time. Just west of the Loch Ness side entry to the mooring, the small island is a *crannog*, made by laying large oak slabs on the lake bottom and holding it in place with stones on top of which a fortification was built. It's a short walk from the mooring up to the bridge and across to St. Benedict's. It's a working abbey, built in 1742 as a fort, and now also houses the **Heritage Center**, a restaurant, and a craft shop. It is certainly worth a visit, as is the town itself. Nice shops and pubs and, for anyone interested in books on Scottish history and good quality crafts, stop by the **Imray Shop**, if only to chat with proprietors Cameron (M.Phil, BA, LLB) and Christine (MSc.) Donnelly. An especially interesting history is *Culloden* (John Prebble, 1996, Bantam Books, London, New York).

After a visit to the **Highlander Exhibition** at the base of the locks, walk along the **Ft. Augustus locks** themselves as a preview to passing your cruiser through them. There are four locks, close together, and a stairway that requires boats to be walked through. By their nature they require some effort, but it is far from daunting. The crew, whether two or eight in number, should be off the boat lending a hand with the lines. There is a lockkeeper who will make sure that all goes well. It's a slow process, harder going up the staircase than down, and requires about an hour. The only difficulty might be for two persons who are operating a large 6-8 berth cruiser, in which case talk to the lockkeeper about assistance. We found other cruiser crew members willing and able to help anyone

Caley Craft cruiser on the Highland Lochs, Ft. Augustus, Invernesshire

who was short-handed. The two of us had no problem with our 35-foot six-berth Highland Commander, although the going was slow. But there is no rush!

Upstream toward the southwest of the Ft. Augustus locks, the next 1½ hour of travel is along the forest-lined canal and **River Oich**, through the attractive **Kytra Lock** with its good moorings (including for overnight), then through **Cullochy Lock** and the **Abercalder Swing Bridge**, both operated by lock keepers, and into **Loch Oich**. This is a slender lake some five miles long with a shallow perimeter along the Cullochy end, well marked (keep red markers on the right while cruising up-lake). This is the "watershed" lake of the system, at an altitude of 106 feet. Toward the northeast, water ultimately flows to the Firth of Moray and North Sea, and to the southwest into salty Loch Linney and the Atlantic.

About half-way along the lake, the ruins of **Invergarry Castle** can seen on a cliff above the right (west) shore. Watch the charts and the red markers carefully to come into the small pontoon mooring at the castle, from where it is an easy walk to the castle and not far in the opposite direction to the **Glengarry Hotel**, and about a mile to the **Invergarry Hotel** for refreshments and, perhaps, a meal. The castle itself was burned in 1746 by Cumberland and his troops after the Battle of Culloden. The walk is worth it, and at the end it offers a grand view of Loch Oich and the Glen.

Fifteen minutes cruising beyond Invergarry along the same shore is the **Well of the Seven Heads**, a monument named for the spot where the heads of seven clansmen were washed clean before being presented to the clan chief. The monument tells the tale. A nice picnic site lies just above one mooring, and a small store where groceries can be bought stands next to the other. This is among several moorings, including Invergarry and Cullochy lock, that are adequate for overnight stops.

Across from the monument is the only truly commercial site

along the lochs: **the Great Glen Water Park**. It comprises a restaurant, lounge, swimming pool, sauna, solarium, laundromat, showers, children's play area, and services like bicycle rental, wind surfing instruction, sailing, waterskiing, and guided hikes. Fortunately, it doesn't meet the standards set by more garish enterprises, whose tall water slides often sully the horizon. It makes for a break from more wild "nature" for those seeking such, and is a good stop if there are children in the crew.

Laggan "Avenue" is simply a two-mile stretch between Loch Oich and Loch Lochy, starting with the **Laggan Swing Bridge** at the northeast. (CAREFUL: The water level changes, so do not attempt to pass without the okay of the keeper who, if it's close, will be standing on the bridge checking clearance). Watch for eagles, and for osprey that by 1916 were extinct in Scotland, but have now returned. It's a lovely stream, ending at the **Laggan Locks** where there is good mooring both above and below the lock gates, a trash disposal, and a pump-out facility if your gauges indicate near full. This is also the boatyard location for **West Highland Sailing**, Crown Blue Line, and the site of the restaurant boat **Sott II**. The marina just beyond the locks on the Loch Lochy side is expansive, with good moorings.

Loch Lochy is the southwestern lake of the chain, a ten-mile-long uninterrupted expanse of easy navigation. The only formal stopping spot is on the east shore about a half-hour cruising from Laggan Lock, where there is a pontoon jetty serving the popular **Letterfinlay Lodge Hotel** (and restaurant). From this stretch of the waterway can be seen the high worn peaks of the **Ben Nevis Range**. The words "Loch Lochy," incidentally, do not translate into "Lake Lakey" as one might expect, but mean "Lake of the Dark Goddess."

The River Lochy empties the lake toward the southwest, and is the last stretch of quiet water before the Caledonian Waterway drops to the sea. The stretch begins at the **Gairlochy Locks**, a pair of lock chambers separated by a swing bridge, and ends some ten miles southwest at Banavie Locks, the end of navigation for fresh-water hire cruisers and sailing yachts.

Also known as **Neptune's Staircase**, Banavie is a series of eight locks close to each other, dramatically dropping the canalized river to sea level across the bay from the city of **Ft. William**. With two sea locks, this marvel of Sir Thomas Telford's engineering makes the waterway possible, allowing access between the sea and the Great Glen and the North Sea beyond. Saltwater-rated cruisers (with larger engines and greater power than the freshwater cruisers) often climb or descend Neptune's Staircase, but for the purposes of this guide, it is the terminus. There is a long quay above the locks with room for many boats to tie up. Ft. William is too far to walk to, and a visit is likely not worth the taxi fare. There is, however, a small general store and post office along the quay if you need provisions. It's a short walk down beside the lock staircase to the **Moorings Hotel** and restaurant toward the right hand, and to the **Lochy Pub** toward the left across the highway and railroad line.

Near Gavolchy Lock, Loch Lochy

Best Times to Go

Thanks to ocean currents Scotland's climate cannot be compared with areas of North America as far north. Generally warmer from autumn through spring than, say, Juneau or northern Quebec, the two important factors to consider in deciding when to go are length of daytime and impact of tourists. As for the former, June is perfect—early sunrise and twilights that last until almost midnight. Being in Scotland, especially on the lochs, during those long summer days is an unequalled delight, bringing to the senses all that natural beauty can offer. Fortunately for Americans whose schools let out in early June, the British schools do not, so family vacation travel to Scotland doesn't really start until late June. Thus, given the factors of weather, season, boat rental prices and tourist traffic, the best times to go are from about May 1 to June 15, and then again between September 5 and October 10. A week earlier and a week later of each period are the second choice, but the risk of inclement weather increases. July and August are the periods of highest boat rental prices, followed by a spike in late May.

The greater the advance booking time, the better the selection of boats. The first to go are the larger cruisers that sleep 6 or more. Play it safe and *for July and August book at least three months in advance*; for *May, early-June and September, two months*; for other times, two to three weeks.

Getting There

The connected chain of Highland lakes that form the Caledonian Waterway lie in the far north of Scotland, some 550 highway miles (890 km) from London. In this sparsely populated part of Great Britain there are few towns, the major center being Inverness, a commercial center easily accessible from virtually all hubs in Great Britain. The best air service from North America is into London-Gatwick or Manchester, then British Airways into Inverness. There are also daily flights in and out of Glasgow.

Rail service is very good, with several departures daily out of London (Kings Cross Station) to Inverness via Edinburgh and Glasgow. More cumbersome are rail connections out of Manchester, but they can be arranged via Blackburn and Carlisle. Contact Rail Pass Express for point-to-point ticketing (Tel: 614-793-7650; Website: www.railpass.com).

As there are only two boat rental companies on the lochs, travel itineraries to them are simple: For travelers without a rental car, by rail or air to Inverness, and on arrival at Inverness, simply travel by airport shuttle and/or taxi to the **Caley Cruisers** boatyard on Canal Road.

Transportation to the other company, **West Highland Sailing**, is more complicated. Its base at Laggan Locks, between Loch Oich and Loch Lochy, is nearer to the southwestern end of the lochs than to Inverness. There are, however, three train departures daily from Glasgow for Ft. William. The 25-mile taxi ride from Ft. William to the boatbase will run about £35. If this is your preference, or if you are already in the vicinity of Ft. William, a good hotel choice is the Nevis Bank Hotel (In the US, call Best Western Tel: 800-528-1234). Arrangements can also be made at the time of booking for transportation from Inverness or Glasgow to the Laggan Lock marina.

We recommend arrival in Britain a day or more before the cruise start day. This is normally Saturday, but with some flexibility in the early and late months of the year. Stay at least one overnight in a hotel or B&B in order to get over jet-lag and to arrive in the vicinity of the boatyard the morning of the departure day. This will give time for grocery shopping, loading luggage, and the hands-on introduction to the cruiser, the charts and the area. If planning to spend the night in Inverness, some centrally located hotel choices are:

- **Crown Hotel**
  Tel/Fax: 1463-231135
  E-mail:crownhotel@aol.com
  www.members.aol.com/crownhotel/scotland.htm

- **The Windsor Hotel**
  Ness Bank
  Tel: 1463-715535, Fax: 1463-713262
  E-mail: info@windsor-inverness.co.uk

- **Dunain Park Hotel**
  Tel: 1463-230512, Fax: 1463-224532
  E-mail: dunainparkhotel@btinternet.com

- **Glenmoriston Town House Hotel**
  20 Ness Bank
  Tel: 1463-223777, Fax: 1463-712378
  E-mail: glenmoriston@cali.co.uk

- **Station Hotel**
  18 Academy Street
  Tel: 1463-231926, Fax: 1463-710705
  E-mail: shi@dial.pipex.com

A complete list can be found at:
http://www.best-hoTel:com/scotland/invernessparttwo

Cruising Time, Cruising Style

None of the hire boat companies on the lochs offers one-way cruising. This means that everything is seen twice, going and returning, so itineraries are based on pace and on things to visit along the way rather than on one-way navigation. The round-trip cruising time between Inverness and Ft. William is approximately 24 hours, assuming no stops at waterside inns, castles, forests, and towns. But of course this defeats the purpose of going to the Highland lochs in the first place. This is a land where there is no hurry, where pleasure can be found in soaking up the scenery while idling along the shoreline or even dropping a fishing line in very deep water. The ideal time for a round-trip, whether a long oval from and to

Inverness or a figure-eight from Laggan Lock, is about a week, figuring the first day begins in the mid-afternoon after familiarization, instruction and stowing luggage and groceries.

A week allows for stops at every main point, and most of the smaller ones along the lochs. This includes time to walk through the choice forests, have lunches and suppers at the lakeshore pubs and restaurants, explore castle ruins, and walk the streets and explore the shops and the Abbey at Ft. Augustus, and to walk down Neptune's Staircase at the Ft. William end.

The alternative way to cruise the Lochs is by sailing yacht out of the West Highland Sailing marina at Laggan Locks. Travel times of course differ when sailing than traveling by motor cruiser. The lakes offer perfect opportunities for sail, and the fleet itself offers a nice choice. Just as for motor cruisers, sailing instruction is available for novices.

Starting at Inverness, cruising southwesterly, the following are the approximate maximum speed, non-stop cruising times between key points along the Caledonian Waterway. To figure longer stretches, just add the consecutive legs. For example, from Inverness to Ft. Augustus is 4½ hours.

Inverness to the start of Loch Ness	1 hr
Start of Loch Ness to Urquhart Castle	1 hr
Urquhart Castle to Foyers	½ hr
Foyers to Ft. Augustus	2+ hrs
Ft. Augustus to Cullochy Lock	1½ hrs
Cullochy Lock to Invergarry Castle	½ hr
Invergarry Castle to Laggan Locks	1 hr
Laggan Locks to Gairlochy Locks	2 hrs
Gairlochy Locks to end of navigation	2 hrs

Don't forget to consider the hours of the locks and swingbridges. There is a 50-minute lunch break daily, sometime between 12–2 PM. Allow a full hour to pass through the Ft. Augustus Locks. Check with the boatyard if your cruising dates are on the fringes of the following general dates:

Early May to Late September: Daily 8 AM–5:30 PM

Early Spring (April) & Autumn (Oct. & Nov.): Daily except Sunday 8 AM–4:50 PM

RENTAL BOAT COMPANY PROFILES

Readers who plan to travel by air or rail to Scotland to cruise the Caledonian Waterway will likely find that Inverness is the best and most convenient starting point. Which means that, unless you are renting sailing yachts, Caley Cruisers is the most convenient boatyard. For sailing, transportation by minibus can be arranged by West Highland Sailing at Laggan Lock from, and to Inverness and Glasgow (about 1½ hours). For convenience, agent contact information appears in Chapter 1 and is repeated at the end of this chapter.

• **Caley Cruisers**
Canal Road
Inverness IV3 8NF
Tel: 1463-236328; Fax: 1436-714879
E-mail: info@caleycruisers.com
Website: www.caleycruisers.com

Caley, pronounced like California, or Caledonian from which the name derives, is a venerable cruiser line that has been owned and operated by the Hogan family for nearly thirty years. A true family affair, everyone seems involved from the founder to the next generation. After traveling a couple of hundred yards down a narrow road alongside the canal to the Caley boatyard, we found a very large operation, dealing not only with the renting and servicing of cruisers, but also the manufacture and outfitting of them. Beside the small reception room/office is a covered dock where the servicing of the cruisers takes place. Next to that is a large building where new cruiser hulls are cradled while being fitted with the latest interiors. These are designed by the family, especially the elder Hogan, every detail from their layout to the nature of the woods, glass, fabrics, knobs, dials, wheel, fridge, cook stove, sink, pumps, diesel engine, and deck rails. We liked this lusty and caring operation, and the fact that the cruisers represented the ideas of the family, which run toward the traditional rather than cold fiberglass and plastic.

The fleet of some fifty cruisers offers a variety of more than a dozen sizes and layouts from the little economy *Lismore* class to the latest addition, the luxury *Highland Monarch*. Of these, seven models, called Caledonian Classics, represent the upper scale boats, all good size cruisers sleeping six to eight comfortably. The other cruisers are all very nice and among the best we've seen for economy cruising. In sum, there is a style for every need and every budget. The *Highland Commander* (sleeps six) that we took was larger than our needs, but we found it easy to manage as well as very comfortable. (Though just the two of us pulling such a large cruiser through the Ft. Augustus Locks was a slow process!) The *Lismore* and *Atlantis* are ideal for two people wanting to cruise economically; the *Sea Chalice* is an excellent choice for two wanting more luxury or for a family of four. We also recommend the *Highland Glen* (four to six people), a slick new cruiser with bow and stern thrusters, and at not much more than the *Highland Commander*.

Getting to the boatyard is a simple matter. A map showing precise directions will be mailed after booking. Just don't assume that because the street along the canal is narrow that it will lead nowhere. It comes to the boatyard less than a quarter-mile from the main road. If arriving by air, take the shuttle into Inverness, then a taxi to the boatyard. (See *Getting There*, above.) If arriving by rail, plan to take a taxi. It is about three miles from the railway station and twelve miles from the airport. Again, if you are just arriving in Britain we suggest coming into Inverness a day early in order to spend the night before starting your adventure. Friday and Saturday start days are typical, although several classes are available on other days. Figure your tentative cruising calendar, then work out your travel plans. The company is flexible except at peak season (July & August) when availability is tight.

Provisioning is also easy. There is a Co-Op supermarket just north and across the bridge from the boatyard, a five-minute drive. If you have no car, transportation to and from the supermarket can be arranged. Groceries are also available along the cruise route at Ft. Augustus, and at the far end of navigation near Ft. William (a small waterside store). Bicycles can be rented and delivered to the boatyard—they are nice to have, but not essential. Same with fishing gear.

The closest mooring for the first night is at Dochgarroch Lock, a tranquil spot just half an hour out, or at Drumnadochit off Urquhart Bay (there is a small fee).

Book directly with Caley Cruisers; major credit cards accepted. Shortly after booking you will receive confirmation and instructions from the Caley agent, Hoseasons Holidays. Or contact Hoseasons if you want their full boating catalog (Tel: 1502-501010; E-mail: mail@hoseasons.co.uk; Website: www.hoseasons.co.uk).

- **Crown Blue Line**
  Laggan Locks, Loch Oich
  Tel: 1603-630513; Fax: 1603-664298
  E-mail: crownhols@dial.pipex.com
  Website: www.crown-holidays.co.uk/
  US: 185 Bridge Plaza North, Suite 310, Fort Lee, NJ 07024
  Tel: 888-355-9491; Fax: 201-242-4476
  E-mail: crownbluelinesus@att.net
  Website: www.crown-blueline.com

This large English-based company specializes in cruising in France, with Ireland, Scotland, The Netherlands, Italy and Germany as secondary markets. It is characterized by large luxury cruisers, medium-size luxury cruisers, and a scattering of those with more modest standards. The prices reflect this, and although class for class their Scotalnd-based boats rent for less than in France, they are higher somewhat than comparable cruisers on the Highland Lochs. They are not for budget boaters, but there is no question that the cruisers are top-notch in terms of design, newness, fitting and equipment. At present there are only three styles available in Scotland from among their large selection, all with 4 to 8 berths. For economy try the *osprey*, but look at the *Braemore*, whose flying bridge affords great views of the countryside.

Their service is enhanced by having an office (not an agent) in the US, making for quick catalog delivery and no time differential.

* **West Highland Sailing**
  Laggan Locks, Span Bridge
  Ft. William, Invernesshire PH34 4EB
  Tel/Fax: 1809-501234
  E-mail: bookings@holidayuk.co.uk
  Website: holidayuk.co.uk/afloat/westhighlandsailing/
      index.htm

Set in one of the most scenic surroundings in Britain, the marina at Laggan Locks is home to a fleet of about eleven motor cruisers and eleven sailing yachts. In operation for some twenty years, this remains an informal operation with a simple reception office sitting beside a substantial marina where a good selection of neat and well maintained boats are berthed.

The 30-foot *Cygnet* is a thoroughly modern cruiser that we recommend for two or a family of four, while the 37-foot *Osprey* class cruiser is a very good choice for four—with a light and airy salon and double berths in separate cabins. For luxury, for four to six, take the *Braemore*, and for value (large cruiser at a modest price) the older, classic *Kingfisher*. We like them all. Except for the little *Beneteau Island 25* (that requires some experience), all the sailing yachts are masthead Bermudan rigged and have diesel auxiliary engines. As noted earlier, the lakes are ideal for sailing. Novices should generally plan an itinerary starting down Loch Lochy from the marina, but specific recommendations will be made during instruction.

Finding the marina is easy for persons driving a rental car, just off the main A82 highway a mile from the hamlet of Laggan; just ask anyone. And transportation to and from either Inverness or Glasgow by minibus can be arranged at the time of booking. It takes about 1½ hours from either and costs approximately £30-35.

Book direct or contact a Blakes agent. Credit cards accepted.

British Agents:

- Blakes Holidays Ltd.
  Tel: 1603-739400; Fax: 1603-782871
  E-mail: boats@blakes.co.uk
  Website: www.blakes.co.uk

- Hoseasons Holidays Ltd.
  Lowestoft, Suffolk NR32 3LT, England
  Tel: 1502-501010; Fax: 1502-586781
  E-mail: mail@hoseasons.co.uk
  Website: www.hoseasons.co.uk

North American Agents for Blakes:

- Great Trips Unlimited
  Tel: 888-329-9720; Fax: 503-297-5308
  E-mail: admin@gtunlimited.com
  Website: www.gtunlimited.com

- Blakes Vacations
  Tel: 800-628-8118; Fax: 847-244-8118
  E-mail: blakes1076@aol.com
  Website: www. blakesvacations.com

North American Agents for Hoseasons & Connoisseur:

- Jody Lexow Yacht Charters
  Tel: 800-662-2628; Fax: 401-845-8909
  E-mail: jlyc@edgenet.com
  Website: www.jodylexowyachtcharters.com

North American Agents for Connoisseur:

- Le Boat
  Tel: 800-922-0291
  E-mail: leboatinc@worldnet.att.net
  Website: www.leboat.com

Appendix

INDEPENDENT BOATYARDS

Some of the following are independent boatyards without agents. From the US first dial 011-44- then the number shown. If dialing from within Britain "0" precedes the town code; for example Wroxham is 01603.

NOTE: An "*" following a company name indicates a boatyard town NOT within easy access of a railroad station (exceeding ten miles).

CHAPTER 2: The Norfolk Broads

North Broads Wroxham/Hoveton Vicinity

Bank Boats*	Smallburgh	1692-582457
Belaugh Boats	Belaugh	1603-782802
Brinkcraft	Wroxham	1603-782333
Brister Craft	Wroxham	1603-783783
Broads Holidays*	Stalham	1692-580748
Broads Tours	Wroxham	1603-782207
Camelot Craft	Hoveton	1603-783096
Compass Craft Ltd	Horning	1692-630401
Ellis Frost Marine Ferry	Horning	1692-630498
Faircraft Loynes	Wroxham	1603-782207
Ferry Boatyard	Horning	1692-630392
Fineway Cruisers Boatyard	Wroxham	1603-782309
George Smith & Sons	Hoveton	1603-782527

Herbert Woods*	Potter Heigham	1692-670711
Horning Pleasurecraft	Horning	1692-630128
Hunter Fleet*	Ludham	1692-678263
John William Boats*	Stalham	1692-580953
Kingline Cruisers	Horning	1692-630297
Ludham Bridge Boat*	Ludham	1692-630486
Ludham Marine*	Ludham	1692-678322
Maycraft Ltd*	Potter Heigham	1692-670241
Moore and Co	Wroxham	1603-783051
New Horizon	Stalham	1692-582277
Phoenix Fleet*	Potter Heigham	1692-670460
Royall & Son Ltd	Hoveton	1603-782743
Sabena Marine	Wroxham	1603-782552
Stalham Yacht Services*	Stalham	1692-580288
Summercraft	Hoveton	1603-782809
Sutton Staithe Boatyard*	Sutton	1692-581653
Urwin Day Boats*	Wayford Bridge	1692-582071
Whispering Reeds Boats*	Hickling	1692-598314
Wroxham Launch Hire	Hoveton	1603-783043

North Broads Middle River Bure

Anchor Craft	Acle	1493-750500
Bridgecraft	Acle	1493-750378
Horizon Craft	Acle	1493-750283/1692-582277
Norfolk Broads Holidays	Acle	1493-751651

South Broads (Norwich area)

Hearts Cruisers	Thorpe St. Andrew	1603-433666/ 1962-582277
Highcraft	Thorpe St. Andrew	1603-701701

| Kingfisher Cruisers | Thorpe | 1692-437682 |
| Maidencraft | Thorpe Norwich | 1603-435173 |

South Broads (Rural/Small Town Boatyards)

Alexander Cruisers	Brundall	1603-715048
Alphacraft	Brundall	1603-713265
Aston Boats (Beccles) Ltd	Beccles	1502-713960
Aston Boats Bridge Street*	Loddon	1508-520353
Bees Boats Riverside Estate	Brundall	1603-713446
Brundall Boat Centre	Brundall	1603-716410
Brundall Marine Centre	Brundall	1603-714744
Buccaneer Boats	Brundall	1603-712057
Castle Craft	St. Olaves/Haddiscoe	1493-488675
Classic Leisure Cruisers	St. Olaves	1493-488675
Fencraft	Brundall	1603-715011
Freshwater Cruisers	Brundall	1603-717355
Gale Cruisers*	Loddon	1508-520300
Hampton Boats	Suffolk	1502-574896
Harbour Cruisers	Brundall	1603-712146
H.E. Hipperson Ltd.	Beccles	1502-712166
Maffett Cruisers*	Loddon	1508-520344
Pacific Cruisers Ltd*	Loddon	1508-520321
Sanderson Marine Craft Ltd.	Reedham	1493-700242
Silverline Marine	Brundall	1603-712247
Swancraft Cruisers	Brundall	1603-712362
Tidecraft Cruisers	Brundall	1603-713348
VIP Harvey Eastwood	Brundall	1603-713345
Willow Cruisers	Brundall	1603-713952

CHAPTER 3: *The Royal Thames*

Ferryline Cruisers	Thames Ditton	208-3980271
Kris Cruisers	Datchet	1753-543930
Maidline Cruisers	Wallingford	149-836088/
		1692-582277
Red Line Cruisers	Oxon	1865-882542
Temple Cruisers	Staines	1784-453433

CHAPTER 4: *Lake Windermere*

Windermere Lake Holidays Afloat	Bowness-on-Windermere	1539-443415

CHAPTER 5: *Other English Waterways*

Bridge Boatyard	Cambridgeshire	1353-663726
Gulliver's Cruisers	Upton-on-Severn	1684-593400
York Marine Services Ltd	Bishopthorpe	1904-704442/
		705815

CHAPTER 6: *Scotland*

Caley Cruisers	Inverness	1463-236328
Crown Blue Line	Loch Oich	1603-630513
West Highland Sailing	Ft. William	1809-501234

For the latest updates to *The Natural Waterways of Great Britain*, visit the book's page on Interlink's website at:
www.interlinkbooks.com/waterwaysGB.html